D1568960

They Don't Have to Die

Home and Classroom Care for Small Animals

Second Edition

by
JIM DUNLAP

Seaside Press

an imprint of Wordware Publishing, Inc.

Library of Congress Cataloging-in-Publication Data

Dunlap, Jim
    They don't have to die : home and classroom care for small animals
    / Jim Dunlap — 2nd ed.
      p.   cm.
    Includes index.
    ISBN   1-55622-533-4 : (pbk.)
    1. Small animal culture.   I. Title.
    SF409.D89   1996
    639—dc21   96-44549
                                          CIP

ISBN 1-55622-533-4
10 9 8 7 6 5 4 3 2 1
A9610

All inquiries for volume purchases of this book should be addressed
to Wordware Publishing, Inc., at the above address. Telephone
inquiries may be made by calling:

(972) 423-0090

TO

My wife Peggy, my daughter
Erin, and my son Scott.

ACKNOWLEDGEMENTS

I would like to thank Elaine Litteral for her contribution of line drawings for this edition. A special thanks to Alan McCuller, not only for his unique cover design, but for the cage and container illustrations. Also, a heartfelt thanks to Martha McCuller for her creativity in page layout and text organization.

Table of Contents

Foreword

As the long-time host of the Wild Kingdom television series, I have been exposed, on a global scale, to man's relationship with animals and our fragile environment. I have seen the deterioration of our planet, oftentimes through mankind's thoughtless, irresponsible actions.

Fortunately, there is a growing sensitivity to the quality of our environment and the creatures that inhabit it. This book is evidence of that trend, and therefore, I highly commend it to parents, teachers, and children.

Specifically, this book deals with acquisition, handling, and treatment of animals, and their effect on our environment. The book tells us how we can borrow animals from nature to study, learn, and benefit. In this process, however, it is important that we return to nature what we take from it. Therefore, we should all be cognizant of the benefits in addition to being sensitive to the potential damage to the animals, our environment, and to ourselves.

I have worked with Jim Dunlap since 1983. I appreciate his concern for the well-being of animals, their habitat, and his missionary-like zeal in teaching others about man's relationship with the animal kingdom. The book's title, *They Don't Have To Die*, both illustrates Jim's concern and aptly summarizes the book's content. This book tells you in practical terms how to borrow from nature in a safe and humane way. After a beneficial encounter with your animal, Jim then tells you how and when you can return it to its home. By using this book, you and your children will develop an enduring appreciation and caring for our animal friends.

Jim Fowler, Host
Wild Kingdom

From the Author

I began collecting, caging, studying, and killing (not on purpose) animals as a young child. Unlike most children, and to my mother's dismay, I never grew out of it. I became a classroom biology teacher, but the urge to collect animals never left. So, I began with one small snake in the classroom and gradually accumulated so many animals that I no longer had room for the kids! After that, the school district built a large building to house my menagerie. The facility is used by students as a hands-on nature lab and an animal library for teachers. I also travel with various animals to the schools in the district for classroom presentations.

About This Book

"A bird in the hand is worth two in the book." That pretty well sums up my philosophy of teaching life science. I found out very early that to motivate, communicate, and educate, the teacher must get the students' attention first. I have used live animals in my classroom from the day I began teaching. I targeted those students in my classes who seemed dead set against learning anything. These students would waltz into class, no books, no paper and no pencil. They would sit at the back of the room, lean back in their chairs, fold their arms, and just dare you to ask them anything. Without a word, I would roll out a cart upon which sat a large trunk. I opened the trunk and pulled out a very large snake, then I waited. The chairs at the back of the room all came down on the floor. All arms unfolded. As I spoke, those dare-to-learn students strained to listen. Then the questions started coming. Is it poisonous? What does it eat? When does it eat? Can I watch it eat? I seized upon their interest by putting some requirements into the privilege of feeding or watching the snake eat. Thus, the first process in educating, getting students' attention, was accomplished. Parents and teachers do not have to have a giant snake, but they can accomplish the same thing with a little knowledge and the use of some easy-to-find resources. A pill bug can be as impressive as an elephant.

This book is designed to help parents, students, and teachers use animals in communication situations without a lifetime commitment to the care and feeding of those animals. We can borrow from nature for short periods of time and take advantage of the magic that takes place between kids and animals and then return the animals without so much as a dent in that delicate balance.

I make strong recommendations as to which types of animals are best suited for each situation, which depends on what you as a parent or teacher plan to accomplish. I recognize the "phases" your children go through when they want to cage and keep anything that breathes. At the end of that "interest" period, there are ways of relinquishing responsibility that are best for the animal and the children involved.

Organization of the Text

Each species' account includes the following information:

Common Name: I have omitted using scientific names because the husbandry is generally the same for closely related animals. For example, the three-toed, ornate, eastern, Florida, and Gulf Coast box turtles all have generally the same requirements.

Acquisition and Handling: Notes on safe capture and holding methods are included in this section. Check this for information about the need for thick gloves in which case you may want to choose a different animal.

Cage and Habitat Materials: Most of the cage suggestions in this section are easy to find, or you can often build or adapt a container that already exists. Much of this material can be found in hardware stores. For each animal in this section I refer to a numbered illustration by figure number. There you will find a line drawing and description with instructions about building materials needed and other information to construct or to locate the appropriate cage.

Although there are many things you can put in the cage to make the animal look comfortable, there are many things you cannot use. This section focuses on those materials that might be detrimental to the health of the animal, as well as those things that are easily obtainable, easiest to clean, and least expensive.

Temperature/Light/Humidity: I have tried to select those animals that will live happily in a room where these factors are the same as for people. There are exceptions that might mean life or death for the animal.

Food and Water: It is necessary to approximate the natural food of each animal to maintain good health. This section describes a variety of diets, and with all captive animals, variety is necessary for good health. Water is necessary for all life but the way it is offered may vary.

Maintenance: Cleaning procedures and frequency are important to natural behavior and health. You can actually do a lot of harm to some animals by keeping them too clean.

Release and Disposal: When and where to release is vital to the animal's survival by taking into account natural habitat, biological clock, age, and other factors. Domestic creatures must find homes with someone who will give at least as much proper care as you did.

Notes and Afterthoughts: Look for tricks of the trade here. I also include some observations from teachers and students who have experience with these animals.

I have included a chapter near the end of the book I refer to as "Sick Call." The health of your animal depends on these factors in this order:

Condition on Acquisition The saddest thing about pet shop animals is that the buyer has no idea of the stress and hardship the animal has undergone since his point of origin and the owner's hands. It is necessary that when you purchase an animal, you look carefully. Ask more questions than you really feel necessary, and see if you can get a guarantee of some kind. Reptiles seem to suffer most from the shipping-crate syndrome. Even if a reptile is deathly ill, he may still hang on for great lengths of time before he dies. This is complicated by the fact that sometimes his appearance is not noticeably changed. Some pet shops feel no obligation to do anything for the animal, and hope for a speedy sale.

General Husbandry When the truth be known, your own cleaning and feeding techniques will result in either an alert and healthy animal, or a sickly, deathbed animal. Clean is always best under any circumstances, the exception being some arachnids, (i.e., spiders, scorpions) that live best in a dirty house (something like a teenager).

Nutrition Try to remember variety in diet is the thread of life. (I think I made that up!) Most meat-eaters will eat veggies and most vegetarians will eat meat, and it is usually necessary for their health. The food must be fresh, clean, and prepared properly (e.g., turtles love carrots but find them hard to eat in their natural shape). You must also be concerned with too much, too little, too frequent, too infrequent, too hot, too cold, and sometimes even the color!

Temperature/Light/Humidity I have had more animals die of dehydration than I've had blow up from too much moisture! Water is essential to life. (I didn't make that up!) Light and quality of light can be critical to some animals, and may be necessary for proper utilization of their nutrients. Heat is a definite factor in the care of most arthropods, reptiles, and amphibians. These animals are poikilothermic (cold-blooded, ectothermic, etc.) that is, their body temperature is regulated by their environment. They must necessarily go an extra step to maintain the optimum temperature, and of course you, as the caretaker, are responsible for allowing them to do this.

Injury Be aware of things in your habitat that might burn, freeze, cut, or fall on your captive. The habitat should be secure on the base, and most handling of the animal should be kept to a minimum.

I am not a veterinarian Veterinary care is sometimes absolutely necessary. There are veterinarians around that do specialize in animals other than dogs and cats. Ask your veterinarian for reference. I will give you the most common symptoms, conditions, and treatment and all others should be attended to by a veterinarian. My grandfather always told me that if I can't help something, at least I shouldn't hurt it.

List of Illustrations

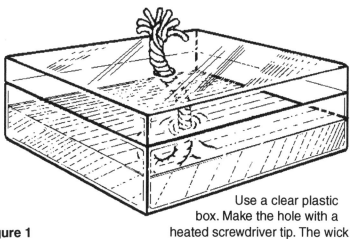

Figure 1
Insect waterer

Use a clear plastic box. Make the hole with a heated screwdriver tip. The wick should be a new cotton rope.

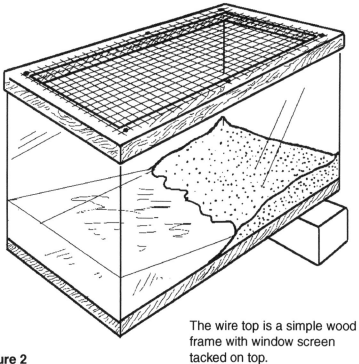

Figure 2
Semi-aquatic habitat

The wire top is a simple wood frame with window screen tacked on top.

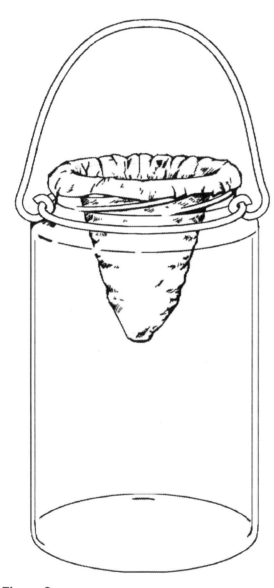

Mold aluminum foil into a funnel and insert into a one-quart wide-mouth jar. Use coat hanger wire to form a hanger and hang under porch light.

Hole in funnel tip should be $\frac{1}{2}$ inch in diameter.

Figure 3
Insect trap

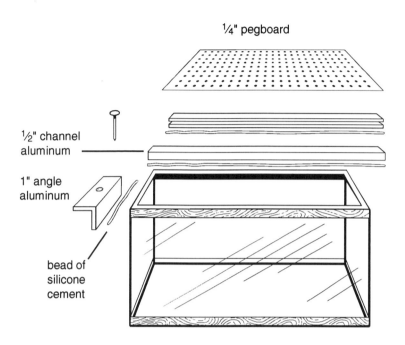

Figure 4
Sliding top aquarium

Instructions for sliding-top aquarium

Materials:
    $\frac{1}{2}$-inch channel aluminum
    1-inch angle aluminum
    silicone cement
    $\frac{1}{4}$-inch pegboard

Use a hacksaw to cut channel aluminum to lengths to fit the top edge of
the long sides of the aquarium. Squeeze a thin bead of silicone along the
top edge (about pencil-lead size). Position channeling on the edge and
press into place with open side of channel to the inside. Cut length of
angle aluminum to fit across the end of the aquarium over the ends of
the channel. Put one bead of silicone on the aquarium frame at the end
of the aquarium. Put one spot of silicone on the end of each channel.
Press angle aluminum into place. Allow to dry for 24 hours. Cut a piece
of 1/4-inch pegboard to fit inside the channeling and one inch longer
than the aquarium. Secure with a bolt through the pegboard and the
angle aluminum.

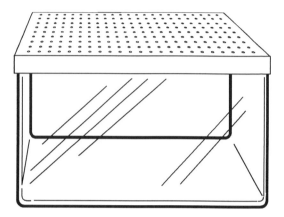

Make air holes in plastic lid by heating a screwdriver tip or large nail (held with pliers) and then melting the holes. Secure lid by melting a hole through lid and box and place a ½-inch stove bolt through the hole.

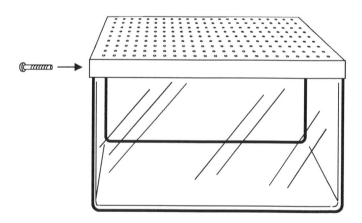

Figure 5
Plastic sweater and shoe storage boxes

Use a nail to punch holes in lid from inside out so as not to expose the inhabitants to sharp edges.

Figure 6
Gallon-jar habitat

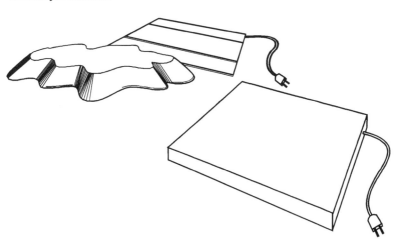

Figure 7
Hot rocks

Check frequently to be sure it is not overheating.

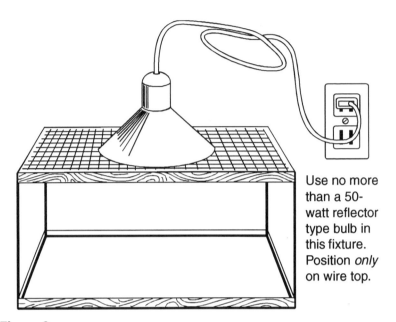

Use no more than a 50-watt reflector type bulb in this fixture. Position *only* on wire top.

Figure 8
Top heat

Top light is optional and decor will vary.

Figure 9
Small reptile habitat

Use a pint or quart jar and no more than a 20-watt bulb.

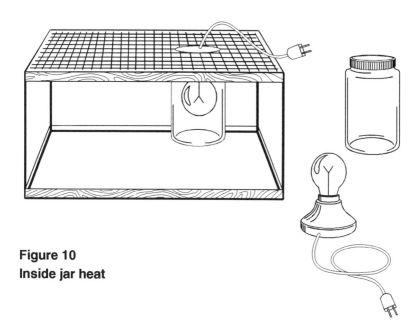

Figure 10
Inside jar heat

Use no more than a 60-watt bulb.

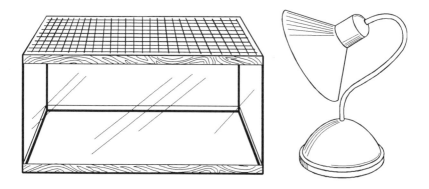

Figure 11
Desk lamp heat

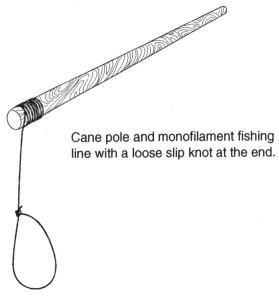

Cane pole and monofilament fishing line with a loose slip knot at the end.

Figure 12
Lizard noose

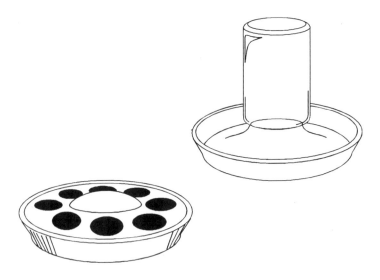

Figure 13
Chick waterer and feeder

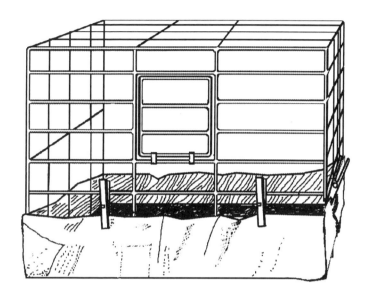

Figure 14
Paper skirt for bird cages

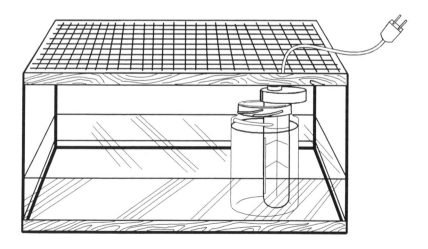

Figure 15
Inside water heater

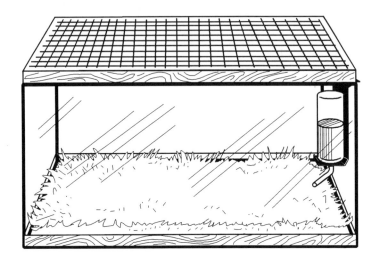

Figure 16
Small mammal habitat

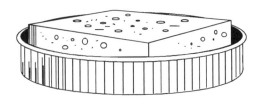

Figure 17
Sponge waterer

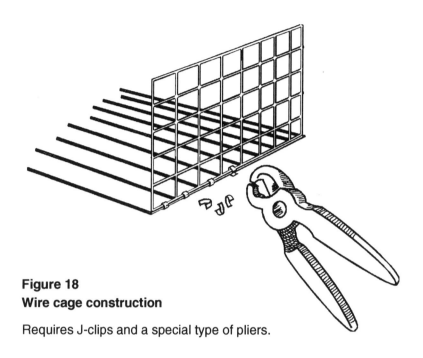

Figure 18
Wire cage construction

Requires J-clips and a special type of pliers.

These are commercially
available and inexpensive.

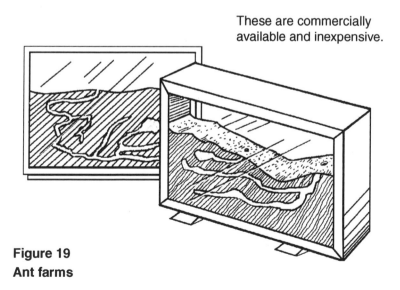

Figure 19
Ant farms

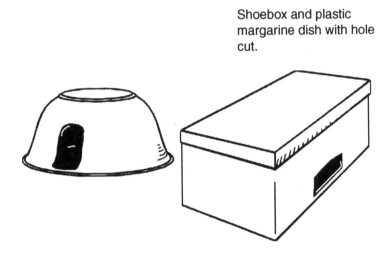

Shoebox and plastic
margarine dish with hole
cut.

Figure 20
Hide boxes for snakes

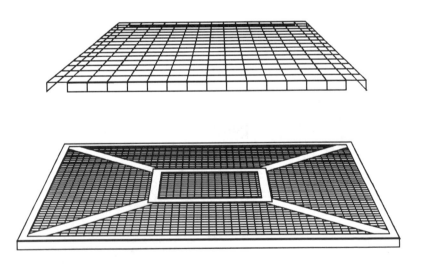

Figure 21
Welded wire and screen tops

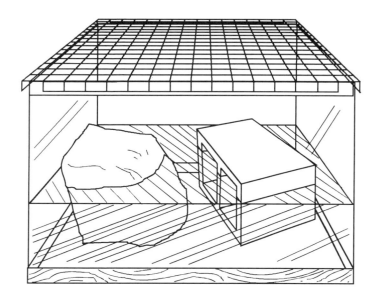

Figure 22
Turtle and frog haul-outs

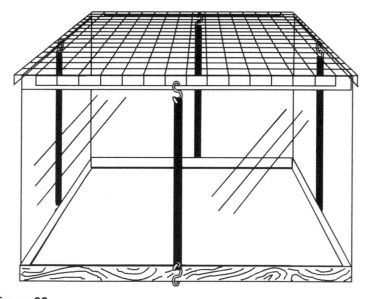

Figure 23
Tie down top

Chapter 1
AMPHIBIANS

Cold-blooded, smooth-skinned vertebrate organisms of the class Amphibia. Characteristically hatching as aquatic larvae that breathe by means of gills and metamorphosing to an adult form having air-breathing lungs.

1

Amphiuma

These are basically eels with two pairs of tiny, useless-looking legs. The backs are black and the bellies are just a little lighter shade. They are completely aquatic but may move occasionally on land and through swamps on rainy nights. Habitats include ditches, ponds, swamps, streams, and almost any permanent body of fresh water. This "swamp thing" is a type of salamander and, therefore, an amphibian. The eggs are laid in water and the hatchlings look like frog tadpoles except for the external gills that appear to be feathers on either side of their heads.

Acquisition and Handling

Their looks will fool you! They bite savagely! If you feel the urge to grab, wear thick gloves or wrap your hand with a few layers of burlap. It is best to use a dip net for capture. You can find them in mud and debris at the water's edge of most area farm ponds.

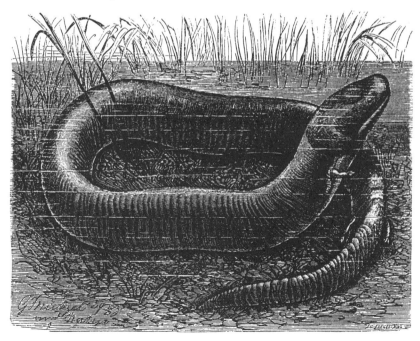

Cage and Habitat Materials

They range in size from 10 inches to 30 inches, so you will need an appropriate-sized aquarium. The best setup is the same as for tropical fish (see fish section), with underground filter, at least four inches of gravel, and a complete top with no openings other than ventilation holes, as they are escape artists. They are air breathers so leave a space between the lid and the top of the water. They really like to hide, so you can half-sink a clay flower pot in the gravel to form a cave.

Temperature/Light/Humidity

Maintain the water temperature at about 75 degrees Fahrenheit, give or take a couple of degrees. Room lighting is sufficient.

Food and Water

In the wild, amphiuma eat worms, insects, small clams, crawfish, small fish, snakes, frogs, and each other! You may purchase feeder guppies or goldfish at the pet store and witness some of the savagery of being wild! Feed at least one or two food items daily. They will also accept commercially produced pellet food. Be sure it is the kind that sinks to the bottom, and only feed what he will eat because the pellet will dissolve and cloud the water.

Maintenance

You will need to change the entire habitat at least once each month. Remove any dead or uneaten foodstuffs at the end of the day. Clean the aquarium with hot water and muscle. Do not use soap. Add water, bottled or treated, as evaporation proceeds.

Release and Disposal

Put him back where you found him! They do hibernate, so be sure to release him during the warmer months to give him time to prepare for bed.

Notes and Afterthoughts

Rule of thumb: one amphiuma per habitat or it could be real nasty! There will be a fight and the loser will become dinner!

African Clawed Frogs

The African clawed frog comes to us through the pet trade. It strikes fear in the hearts of biologists all over the United States because it is almost impossible to destroy and it is very destructive to our native fauna. It eats fish, fish eggs, aquatic larvae, and just about anything else smaller than it and that doesn't bite back! The clawed portion of the name is a misnomer because, as with all amphibians, they do not have claws. They do, however, have long thin fingers that resemble claws.

Acquisition and Handling

They are inexpensive and may be purchased from your local pet shop. They can also be mail-ordered from most children's magazines. Handling is almost impossible because of their slick mucus coat and the fact that they never sit still. All handling should be kept to a minimum because when this mucus coating is interrupted, it may set up a site for infection.

Cage and Habitat Materials

I keep my clawed frogs in a 10-gallon aquarium with about four inches of spring water. This way, it is not necessary to use a lid or cover as these frogs cannot escape. If you prefer a more elaborate habitat, you can set up a 10-gallon aquarium much as you would for tropical fish (see instructions in the fish section). When the water level is to the top take care that the cover or lid is always secure, because these frogs will leave. Allow for space between the bottom of the cover and the top of the water for breathing room.

Temperature/Light/Humidity

Maintain a water temperature of between 75 to 80 degrees Fahrenheit. In the fish aquarium setup, this may be accomplished with a standard aquarium heater. If you use the four-inches-of-water-and-nothing-else method, you may use the heat setup shown in Fig. 15. Room lighting will suffice.

Food and Water

Commercially prepared fish pellets, dried bloodworms, shrimp pellets, Reptomin, and some others will do quite nicely. You may also feed them small bits of lean meat or liver; and they really like insects such as moths, grasshoppers, and other critters you can catch with your insect trap shown in Fig. 3. Feed them four times a week at least two or three food items.

Maintenance

Remove all uneaten food if it is not accepted almost immediately. The underground filter of the fish aquarium setup

will keep the water clean for a long time. The four inches of water setup will need to be changed at least once each week. Always use treated or bottled water when you change or add.

Release and Disposal

Try friends, teachers, and then the pet shop. A population of these animals in any of our waterways is biologically disastrous. This is hard to say, but the best thing to do is to put the frog in a plastic container and let him spend the night in the freezer! This is humane disposal because, being cold blooded, they simply lapse into a deep and deeper sleep.

Notes and Afterthoughts

Although they don't have jaw strength or teeth to hurt you, they will grab a pointed finger, which usually means you have an airborne, injured frog!

Bullfrogs

These are the largest of the American frogs — measuring up to eight inches from nose to rear. You can add another eight inches for legs. They come in shades of color from green to brown. They love shallow water with lots of vegetation. They are the world's champion jumpers and can flatfoot over 15 feet. You may witness some of this as you approach a pond and hear a loud croak and a soon-to-follow splash. The females lay their eggs in late February or early March some 20,000 at a time. The tadpoles transform slowly and may take up to two years to develop into frogs.

Acquisition and Handling

Unless you are quick with a net and very lucky, you might
want to look for these jumping across the road at night
after a rain. They can sometimes be cut off if you can get
between them and the water. Look in the short marsh grass
at the water's edge. They should be grasped around the
waist just in front of the back legs, and you must hold on.
Each time you handle the frog be prepared to give chase!

Cage and Habitat Materials

You should have a 30-gallon aquarium or larger because
they need space. Fill the tank to a depth of four inches.
Place a large flat-topped rock at one end of the tank. The
rock surface should be just above the water as illustrated in
Fig. 22. A secure top is necessary. Use the plastic and screen
top as shown in Fig. 21 with the screw down attachment.
You may use a welded wire top if it is secured with a stretch
cord around the middle of the aquarium (see Fig. 23).

Temperature/Light/Humidity

The water temperature should be between 75 and 80
degrees Fahrenheit. This may be accomplished using the
heating method shown in Fig. 8. Room lighting will be
sufficient.

Food and Water

Use creek or bottled water to avoid chemical contamination. Bullfrogs will eat just about anything that is smaller
than they are. Try cicadas, June beetles, crickets (a lot of
them!), or, how do I say this — a small live mouse! Place
the food items on the flat rock. Leave it only for an hour or
so. Feed daily as many items as he will eat.

Maintenance

Change the water as it becomes clouded. Do not allow
uneaten food to foul the water.

Release and Disposal

Release the animal where you found him or in a similar
habitat. They do hibernate so release them during the
warmer months.

Notes and Afterthoughts

It is difficult to get these animals to feed. One condition
you might try is to make the habitat dark and quiet.

Cricket Frogs

These little frogs are those you see only for a moment. They jump from the bank into the water and then swim back to the shore. Then they look up at you with those big sad froggy eyes to see what you'll do next.

Acquisition and Handling

Cricket frogs can be grabbed by a very energetic third grader. They can also be snagged by sweeping a butterfly net just across the grass at the water's edge. They should not be handled unless necessary as they are fragile.

Cage and Habitat Material

A 10-gallon aquarium will house three to five frogs. You can decorate the habitat with branches and flat rocks. The semi-aquatic habitat shown in Fig. 2 is just right for cricket frogs. The small animal habitat illustrated in Fig. 9 will do with a little reorganization. For this setup just a large shallow water pan with a flat rock in the center will do. Keep in mind that they hide for a living, so if you want to see them, use less decor.

Temperature/Light/Humidity

Cricket frogs do well at room temperature and light. Watch the water level and refill regularly.

Food and Water

Cricket frogs eat very small live insects. You may purchase baby crickets at the pet store or bait shop. You may catch insects using the trap shown in Fig. 3. Feed about two insects per frog per day. Remove all uneaten food at the end of the day.

Maintenance

Change and clean the habitat as often as the water clouds. Use only hot water and elbow grease to clean. Use bottled or creek water for all changes and additions.

Release and Disposal

Release the frogs where you collected them if possible. If not, seek a similar habitat and climate. They hibernate, so release them during the warm months.

Notes and Afterthoughts

If you keep them over winter, be sure to maintain a constant water temperature. You must also locate a winter insect supply. If you can't find them at the pet shop or bait store, try calling your local college or high school biology department for a source of wingless fruit flies. Don't over-crowd. Put no more than five frogs in a 10-gallon aquarium.

Grass Frogs

Frogs are truly wonderful animals. The stories and myths surrounding them revolve around their powerful voices and shocking appearances which give rise to superstitions in every culture. Yet frogs are interesting animals to watch and to learn from, since they progress through many different stages of metamorphosis, each one distinctly unique. You cannot get warts from frogs or any other amphibians. Some species can leave an irritating rash or burning sensation if they do contact your skin. We won't talk about the poison arrow frogs from South America that can kill you. Frogs are amphibians and most of them require water for reproduction.

Acquisition and Handling

Capture is difficult. They move fast and are wary of predators. An insect net may be used to trap them against the ground. Search marshy areas because in deep water they simply can't be caught. To hold, grasp them firmly about the hips and hold on. Frogs should not be handled unless you plan to kiss them hoping for a prince! Handling breaks a protective mucus covering of their skin and sets up sites for infection.

Cage and Habitat Materials

For one frog, use a plastic sweater box or something similar (see illustration, Fig. 5). Be sure to use the bolts to secure the lid. Fill with about one inch of spring water or treated aged water. You can use sphagnum moss or flat stones to construct an island at one end of the container so the frog can crawl out occasionally.

Temperature/Light/Humidity

Keep the frog in a constant room temperature. Avoid direct sunlight for extended periods of time as it can dry out their skin quickly. Room lighting will suffice.

Food and Water

Frogs prefer live insects. You can use the insect trap shown in Fig. 3. They enjoy crickets, mealworms, earthworms and small insects. Avoid feeding residential crickets and grass-hoppers as they tend to store insecticides and may kill your frog. Feed your frog at least two or three food items daily. Put the food on the island and remove uneaten food at the end of the day. You can purchase grey crickets at the bait shop.

Maintenance

Change the water at least every third day. Most frogs secrete a toxic chemical that in concentration might kill the frog. Do not use soap when cleaning. Wash your hands after cleaning the habitat or after necessary handling of the frog because the mucus from their skin can cause a rash.

Release and Disposal

Return the frog to its natural surroundings where you originally picked it up, or in similar habitat, before the cold weather sets in.

Notes and Afterthoughts

A good rule of thumb is one frog per habitat.

Newts

Common newts sold in pet shops are totally aquatic although they do go through a stage that other salamanders do not. First they are larvae which look like tadpoles with feather-looking gills sticking out of their heads and then they grow legs and become adults. The common newts have a third phase — the tadpoles hatch, eat, grow, and turn into a very bright red. During this time they go through a short land-dwelling phase before becoming totally aquatic and returning to the water.

Acquisition and Handling

Most pet shops sell newts. If you frequent the moist forested areas of their natural habitat, you may be lucky enough to turn over a wet log or some wet leaves and find one. They really should not be handled as they are very fragile and susceptible to infections.

Cage and Habitat Materials

The standard fish aquarium of whatever size is sufficient for a newt. They enjoy hiding places so provide a small flower pot or something similar buried in the gravel to form a small cave. It is not necessary for them to have a surface out of the water. Look at the section on fish for instructions to set up a simple aquarium.

Temperature/Light/Humidity

The aquarium water should be between 73 and 78 degrees Fahrenheit. The standard aquarium light will do; be sure to turn it off at night to avoid excess algae growth.

Food and Water

Newts eat almost any small insect; you can float two or three baby crickets at the water surface and they can catch them. They will also eat pelleted fish food that will not float. Do not overfeed — they should be fed about every other day. The pelleted food will be attacked and swallowed usually before it hits the bottom. Do not feed them meal-worm larvae because they cannot digest the exoskeleton. This may cause intestinal blockage and death.

Maintenance

Remove all uneaten food by the day's end and keep one or two scavenger fish, such as the Cory catfish, and a few pond snails to control algae. A full water change may be required occasionally; be sure to use either aged water or water that has been treated to remove the ammonia and chloramines. Refer to the section on fish setup. Newts are sensitive to chemicals found in tap water.

Release and Disposal

When you are through with them, call these people (not necessarily in this order): your student's teacher, the local nature center, your local city aquarium, or any tropical fish breeder. Do not release the animals into local waterways because that will mean certain death! If they were collected in the forest, return them to the forest.

Notes and Afterthoughts

Newts may be kept with other tropical fish, but be careful about fish that nip little feet!

Small-mouthed Salamanders

Small-mouthed salamanders are five to seven inches long, dark gray or black, and dinky-legged. As the name implies, they have tiny mouths and a small clown-like face. They are not the most desirable classroom or household pet because they are so secretive you hardly ever see them.

Acquisition and Handling

These salamanders are semi-terrestrial and require only moist soil to exist. They may be found in dirt or leaf litter beneath logs, rocks, and other debris found near ponds or lakes. They don't bite but should not be handled because of their protective mucus skin covering that, when disturbed, sets up an infection site.

Cage and Habitat Materials

A 10-gallon aquarium, plastic shoe box, or sweater box will do nicely. See the illustration in Fig. 2 and Fig. 5. There are two setups depending upon the length of time you anticipate keeping these animals. The first is one to two inches of aquarium gravel with water level kept even with the gravel surface at all times. Supply a flat rock or piece of bark for hiding. The other setup is one to two inches of sandy loam kept wet to the point of almost mud. Cover with a thin layer of dead leaves.

Temperature/Light/Humidity

These salamanders do best in cooler temperatures from 65 to 75 degrees Fahrenheit. Available light will suffice and high humidity is required.

Food and Water

Small-mouthed salamanders eat a variety of small insects and worms. These can be supplied by use of the insect trap as shown in Fig. 3. Worms can be found under rocks or logs in wet areas or by digging in moist soil beneath leaf litter. One or two food items daily should be offered. Keep the habitat wet at all times. Even a few minutes of dryness will kill these salamanders.

Maintenance

The aquarium gravel water substrate should be changed about every two weeks. Always use bottled or creek water for replacement. The dirt and leaf substrate should be changed more often as it is likely to stagnate, smell bad, and may become toxic to your captive. Do not use soap to clean the habitat, just hot water and elbow grease.

Release and Disposal

Release these animals in the early fall to allow them time to prepare for hibernation. Try to release them in the area where they were collected.

Notes and Afterthoughts

Keep the habitat as uncluttered as possible so you will be able to view your captives more frequently.

Tadpoles

The neat thing about keeping tadpoles is that you can fish them out of the creek, watch them develop, and then put the frogs and toads back into the creek! Frogs and toads start out as tadpoles and develop in very similar ways, so identification early on is not really necessary. The only problem that might arise is that bullfrog tadpoles may take two years to develop into frogs. As a general rule of thumb, the toad tadpoles are very small and black. Frog tadpoles are shades of green and longer than one inch.

Acquisition and Handling

Check out any shallow, clear, standing water. Watch for marbles with tails and be quick with a dip net! Tadpoles should not be handled as they have a protective mucus coating that, if disturbed, might allow a bacterial infection to develop.

Cage and Habitat Materials

A plastic sweater box as shown in Fig. 5 makes a great tadpole farm. Fill with water to a depth of two inches; the
water should come from the creek or be chemically treated
to remove chlorine and chloramines. Aged aquarium water
will do nicely if you have some on hand. As your tadpoles
develop, you will need to add flat rocks to allow the young
frogs or toads to come out of the water.

Temperature/Light/Humidity

Tadpoles develop well in available light. The water temperature should be between 72 and 75 degrees Fahrenheit. Use
the water heater setup shown in Fig. 15.

Food and Water

Tadpoles are omnivorous and may be fed goldfish food,
boiled spinach or kale, mashed hard-boiled eggs, or
chopped liver. Their natural food consists of the algae
growth on rocks and water plants. To grow algae in your
habitat place it near a window where sunlight will facilitate
algae growth.* Food should be offered daily and removed
after an hour or so to avoid fouling the water. If the water
turns cloudy, they are being overfed and are not consuming
all the food. You can make adjustments as necessary. When
the legs have developed and the tail is being absorbed, the
young frogs will not eat as much. They are developing feeding habits from dead stuff to live stuff! As they stay on the
rocks more frequently, they will need to be offered live
insects such as small crickets and insects that you capture
in your back porch trap, as shown in Fig. 3. Your habitat at
this point should begin to look like the illustration in Fig. 2
— half water and half substrate. If fed too little they may
begin to eat each other.

* Do not put habitat in direct sunlight because the water
will overheat and boil your captive.

Maintenance

Change water as needed. A lot of tadpoles go out with the wash, so be careful. Don't use tap water because they absorb chemicals through their skins. Clean the habitat with hot water and muscle.

Release and Disposal

Simply put them back in or near the body of water where you found them. Release during the warm months as they do hibernate.

Notes and Afterthoughts

It takes ten to fourteen weeks to grow from tadpole to frog or toad, so be patient!

Tiger Salamanders

These are the biggest land dwelling salamanders in the world. They like dark, damp places. They breed in small ponds. The tadpoles look like frog tadpoles, except for the gills which are external and look like feathers on either side of their heads. These gills disappear as the salamander develops into an adult. They may grow to a foot long when mature.

Acquisition and Handling

Tiger salamanders can be collected in their habitat by looking beneath logs, flat stones, or human debris such as boards and pieces of tin around or near any body of water. They are very slick and must be handled carefully and gently. They can and do bite but their serrated-edge teeth are not long enough to break the skin. In some areas around recreational lakes they can be purchased in bait shops. The bass love 'em!

Cage and Habitat Materials

The 10-gallon aquarium is a suitable habitat for these salamanders. The substrate should be pea gravel or aquarium gravel to a depth of about an inch. To this, you add spring water or treated water to a depth of one inch. Provide a flat stone for a place to haul out. Look at the setup in Fig. 2. These salamanders are climbers, so a secure top is necessary. I suggest, to avoid escape and to hold in humidity, use a plate of glass over the top of the aquarium. Place multilayers of tape in each corner to allow for air passage.

Temperature/Light/Humidity

Salamanders prefer the cooler side of the temperature range and should be between 60 and 80 degrees Fahrenheit. Temperatures exceeding 86 degrees Fahrenheit will kill the animals. They prefer semi-darkness and do very well in cool shaded spots.

Food and Water

Aquatic amphibians are guided as much by odor as by movement in finding food. They will eat bits of meat, worms, or dead fish as well as live prey, such as crickets, grasshoppers, and worms. They should be fed once each day and only as much as they will eat at one time. Remove all uneaten food so as not to foul the water.

Maintenance

The aquarium should be dismantled and thoroughly cleaned once each week using only hot water and a paper towel. The gravel should be rinsed thoroughly and changed completely when algae and other scum builds up.

Release and Disposal

Try to release the animal in the same spot where you collected him. If this is not possible, try to replicate the habitat of origin. Do not release in late fall or during the winter.

Notes and Afterthoughts

All amphibians secrete toxins through their skin which can actually be harmful to themselves if there are too many individuals in the tank or if the water is not changed regularly. Two to three medium-sized salamanders per 10-gallon tank is a good rule of thumb. This means change the water frequently.

Toads

Toads are representative of the class of animals known as amphibians, along with salamanders, frogs, and newts. These amphibians spend part of their time in the water for reproduction and the rest of their lives on land. They are sometimes known as true toads and they do have warts. These warts are really oil glands to keep the skin moist, and they cannot pass them along to people. Toads eat just about anything that moves and is smaller than they are, and they enjoy burying themselves in the dirt until they show up around feeding time. Toad tadpoles differ from frog tadpoles in that they are much smaller and usually all black. They develop in the same way as frogs, and when they climb out on land, they do not return to water except to lay eggs.

Acquisition and Handling

Toads may be obtained on any warm summer evening near any body of water and are usually attracted to light. The reason is that insects are also attracted to light and they come there to dine. You need only to stroll through a neighborhood park armed with a flashlight and you will find them hopping across the sidewalk. You should pick up a toad at first by grasping him on either side of the backbone and simply lifting him up. After a moment you can cradle him in your hands for more security. The reason for this is that they have a rather odd way of protecting themselves — they urinate very freely when picked up. So, it is better to let them get that out of the way before you handle them. You should also be sure that you wash your hands after handling them because they do have a mucus covering on their skins that is very bitter to the taste and sometimes has an irritating effect on human skin.

Cage and Habitat Materials

The good old 10-gallon aquarium makes an excellent habitat for the toad. You can fill it with three to four inches of
topsoil and provide a hiding place such as a small flat rock
or something that the toad can dig beneath. They do enjoy
burying themselves in the dirt and seem to be most healthy
when they are allowed to do that. A wire top can be
provided; most toads are not capable of jumping out of a
10-gallon aquarium, but it is always better to be safe. Look
at setups and tops in Fig. 2 and Fig. 21.

Temperature/Light/Humidity

Toads do well at room temperature with available light. It is
very important to not let the toad's environment become
too dry. Keep the soil moist, not wet. Keep a water dish
available so the toad has a place to soak and absorb
moisture. Mist the habitat with a plant atomizer about
three times each week to keep the humidity high.

Food and Water

Toads feed primarily on insects and other small inverte-brates. They must be alive, since it is the movement that attracts the toad's attention. Insects that crawl or walk are easier for the toad to catch than those that leap or fly. Mealworms, crickets, and earthworms make excellent food. These animals can be purchased at a pet shop or some are available at bait shops. Feed the toad by dropping these things into the cage. Sometimes the toad can be tricked into eating other foods. I have had success with small, round, semi-moist cat food bits. I simply place them on the cage floor in front of the toad and then I take a long, thin wire and "tickle" the food so that it moves. Feed them three to five food items each day. They will love the insects you catch in the insect trap shown in Fig. 3.

Water can be provided in a bowl that is not too deep and big enough so that the toad can immerse his entire body into the water.

Maintenance

The entire habitat should be dismantled and completely cleaned at least every two weeks. The water bowl should be removed, cleaned, and refilled daily. All uneaten food should be removed at the end of the day. Insect carcasses have a tendency to build up and cause various kinds of fungal and bacterial growths that may be harmful to your captive.

Release and Disposal

Toads hibernate. Therefore, they are best suited for being captive pets from early spring through summer. They should be released in early fall so they can prepare for hiber-nation. If you choose to keep one through the winter, it is necessary to maintain a constant temperature and time of light cycle. The ideal temperature is between 75 and 80 degrees Fahrenheit.

Notes and Afterthoughts

Once a month or so the toad's skin will take on a glassy
appearance and he will hunker down on the bottom of the
aquarium. There's no problem here; that is the first stage of
skin shedding. Watch and ooh!

Tree Frogs

These little frogs, one to two inches long, are usually bright green, but the color is variable and they may be nearly yellow or a dull slate gray. You will hear them singing to the top of their voice sacs during the spring and especially after a rain. They are sometimes known as rain frogs but that also applies to a number of other different species. They like swamps, borders of lakes and streams, and floating vegetation. They are attracted at night by lights where they find the insects they love to eat.

Acquisition and Handling

Don't handle them! They are far too fragile for fondling. They are best captured with a small insect or fish net. Finding them is the most difficult part because they will blend in with the surroundings. The experts can locate them by their sound, and you can try that if you're an expert! One technique is to squat down and look at the marsh foliage from beneath — very carefully.

Cage and Habitat Materials

The plastic sweater box, as shown in Fig. 5, is best for these animals because when they are not adhering to the branches, they will lodge themselves in an available corner. Crisscross the container with branches and you might add a potted green plant or two; they will love them. The substrate can be about one inch of aquarium or pea gravel.

Temperature/Light/Humidity

They prefer the cooler side of the range between 70 and 80 degrees Fahrenheit; they do well in available light and prefer high humidity. You can adjust the number of air holes in the sweater box lid to achieve a slight condensation on the inside at all times.

Food and Water

Keep the habitat in standing water at all times. Be sure to use bottled or creek water to avoid toxins. Tree frogs eat live insects which you can catch with the insect trap shown in Fig. 3. Offer two or three insects each day and remove uneaten insects at the end of the day.

Maintenance

Change and clean the entire habitat at least once each week. Do not use soap or cleaner. Hot water and elbow grease should do it. Do not use an abrasive scrubber on the plastic as it will scratch and cloud the container. Wash the gravel thoroughly with each change.

Release and Disposal

Release the animals in or near the place you collected them. Let them go in the warm months before the first frosts as they need to find a place to hibernate.

Notes and Afterthoughts

Two frogs per plastic shoe box is a good rule.

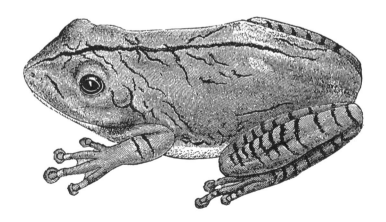

Chapter 2
ARACHNIDS
Diplopods
Chilopods

Arachnids: Arthropods of the class
Arachnida. Characteristically having four
pairs of legs.

Diplopods: Segmented, cylindrical
arthropods of the class Diplopoda, which
includes the millipedes.

Chilopods: Arthropods of the class
Chilopoda, which includes the centipedes.

Centipedes

The centipede is not an insect and is not an arachnid. These creatures are of the class Chilopoda, which when translated means one pair of legs per each segment of their bodies. There are over 3,000 species of centipedes, so we will be very general in the descriptions. Most are nocturnal. During the day they hide under rocks, leaves, or loose bark. They avoid extremely wet or dry places. They are carnivorous, feeding mostly on insects and worms, but they will consume a lizard or small snake if they can catch it. All have poison glands opening through their jaws, and the ferocious bite can cause extreme pain but usually is not dangerous. Grandmother, bless her heart, tells us that if the centipede crawls across your skin, you will rot everywhere a foot touches. Not true, but think twice before grabbing one of these.

Acquisition and Handling

Centipedes can be found in fields, forest, vacant lots, under stones, logs, boards, and other debris. To catch one, place a cup or glass jar over the centipede and slip an index card between the jar and the ground. Attempting to grab the animal with tweezers could result in grave injury to the centipede and a painful bite for you.

Cage and Habitat Materials

The plastic shoe box illustrated in Fig. 5 makes an excellent home for your centipede. The substrate used can be dirt, sand, newspaper, ground corn cobs, or aquarium gravel. Pieces of flat bark or toilet paper rolls should be provided for hiding places. Keep one end of the habitat slightly moistened; particularly under the hiding place.

Temperature/Light/Humidity

These animals become dormant at low temperatures and do well at room temperature with standard room lighting.

Centipedes enjoy humid places, so mist the substrate about twice a week.

Food and Water

Water should be provided with the insect waterer illustrated in Fig. 1. Centipedes are carnivorous and thrive on insects. The insects can be trapped using the insect trap illustrated in Fig. 3. A good maintenance diet is one insect per day.

Maintenance

As hard as it is to understand, the key to successful centipede keeping is to not clean the cage at all. They seem to do well in their own untouched surroundings. Remove uneaten food at the end of the day. Change and clean waterer as needed.

Release and Disposal

The ideal release is to let the centipedes go at the place you found them and during the same season you found them. If this is not possible, then release them in the same general area, before the first frost.

Notes and Afterthoughts

These animals have a ferocious bite. They do have sharp appendages at the end of the tail which will stick if you pin the animal down. They live about two or three years.

Safety note: Secure the lid of the shoe box with screws placed in holes in the ends of the box. You might also put a strong rubber band around each end of the box. Place the habitat on a sturdy table and well away from the edge. Watch little fingers!

Daddy Long-legs Spiders (Harvestmen)

There are many different species of these spiders; they are most recognizable because of their extremely long legs and their very small bead-like body. They construct loose webs in dark corners of out buildings or cellars. Males and females are commonly found together and seem to get along just fine.

Acquisition and Handling

These creatures may be found in almost any outdoor corner, under the eaves of houses and, especially during summer camp, they can be found grouped in the corners of outhouses and walking across dry leaves in low-lying moist areas. Grabbing one by the leg will usually cause it to break off. The easiest method of capture is to place a wide-

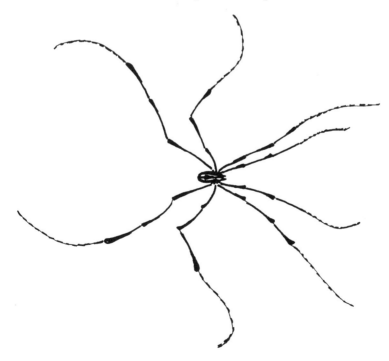

mouthed can, such as a coffee can, on the ground and use a twig to coax the animal inside. All spiders bite and this one will if he can get a good angle. The pain is no worse than a bee sting unless you have allergies.

Cage and Habitat Materials

The larger the better. The 10-gallon aquarium makes a nice habitat for the daddy long-legs. The substrate should be an inch or two of rich soil covered with a thin layer of dry leaves. A screen top is best to prevent escape. See the illustration in Fig. 21. They enjoy vertical surfaces, so a flat board such as a wood shingle leaning against the side will be used and enjoyed.

Temperature/Light/Humidity

These spiders do well at room temperature and available light. Humidity is of some importance, not too moist and not too dry. Mist the inside of the habitat about once each day.

Food and Water

The daddy long-legs feed mainly on living insects. The smaller the better. These insects may be captured in your insect trap as shown in Fig. 3. They are known to also eat carrion, that is, dead animals or plant juices. It may be best to also offer fresh, live branches which should be replaced every other day or so. Feed one insect every three to five days. Water may be supplied by the sponge and lid setup as shown in Fig. 17.

Maintenance

Remove all uneaten food at the end of the day. It may be occasionally necessary to sponge down the inner surfaces of the aquarium as the spider will walk around and perhaps spread the dirt here and there. Change the water sponge at least twice a week.

Release and Disposal

Try and release the animal in the area where he was captured. If this animal was obtained from summer camp that might be difficult, so any outlying area where there are fields and tall grasses will be sufficient.

Notes and Afterthoughts

Most species of the daddy long-legs do not live for more than a year; consequently, that should be considered and the animal should be released very soon after capture.

Garden Spiders, Argiope

These large (four inches across) yellow and black spiders build a large web and spin a squiggly ribbon of white in the center. They are found throughout the United States and they seem to prefer sunny sites with little or no wind. When disturbed, they drop to the ground and hide.

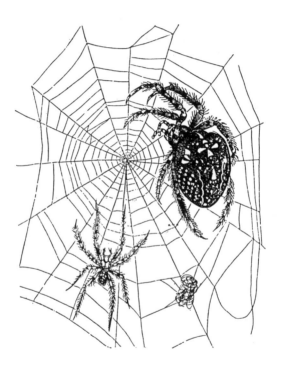

Acquisition and Handling

If you are lucky enough to find one of their elaborate webs on the school grounds or in your backyard, tell the kids you are declaring the spot a "Federal Natural Area," then protect it and observe. If you must bring them inside, they are easily herded into a coffee can or similar wide-mouthed container by using a small twig. They do bite, so be careful. The bite is the equivalent of a bee sting.

Cage and Habitat Materials

Keep in mind that this will be a temporary setup for only a few days. A 10-gallon aquarium or larger with a wire top will be needed. Use one inch of soil or gravel for the substrate. Place long twigs at each end of the aquarium from bottom to top. This will provide a location for a web to be constructed.

Temperature/Light/Humidity

Place the habitat near a window for warmth. Room temperature and humidity will suffice.

Food and Water

Argiope eat small insects that you can trap in your back porch light trap as shown in Fig. 3. If you are lucky and your spider builds a web, you can toss the insect into the web and watch him in action. Feed the spider one or two insects every other day. Offer water with the sponge and lid setup shown in Fig. 17.

Maintenance

Keep the sponge moist but avoid getting the spider wet, as this may cause health problems. Remove dead and uneaten insects from the habitat at the end of each day.

Release and Disposal

Set them free in about the same place where you caught them, preferably within a few days of capture.

Notes and Afterthoughts

The female argiope may live five to ten years, whereas the male may last only one or two seasons. Occasionally, the male's life ends abruptly when, after mating, the female decides he is a food item!

House Spiders

Grandfather always told me that small, long-legged spiders magically appeared in every dark corner of the house. When I need one for something, I just look under a table leg and one will pop up. Although they don't magically appear, house spiders are very common and are usually found somewhere in the house regardless of how hard you try to keep them out. House spiders have a pea-sized body and thin legs about an inch long. They make an irregular web that resembles the dust wisp caused by long-standing dust accumulation.

Acquisition and Handling

I've already mentioned where you can find them; and like all spiders, they can bite if they can get the angle. It's best to herd them into a small container using a small stick or broom straw.

Cage and Habitat Materials

The shoe box or sweater box shown in Fig. 5 will do nicely as a spider cage. A substrate is not really necessary, and you can crisscross the container with small twigs. Take care not to make the air holes in the top of the container so large that the spider can escape.

Temperature/Light/Humidity

Room temperature, light, and humidity will suffice. That's the big reason they are called house spiders.

Food and Water

House spiders feed mainly on living insects, the smaller the better. You can capture insects in the insect trap shown in Fig. 3. Feed one insect each week. These spiders are not tough enough to overstuff! Water may be supplied by the sponge waterer shown in Fig. 17.

Maintenance

Remove uneaten insects at the end of the day so the food won't eat the spider! After the spider's established, don't clean the container! Change to a new sponge about once a week.

Release and Disposal

They will survive outside, and that's a good place to put them.

Notes and Afterthoughts

These spiders do not get along well with their relatives so put one spider per habitat.

Jumping Spiders

Jumping spiders are members of the group of hunting spiders that pursue and attack prey. They are small, dime size, furry, black and have a small white dot on their backs. These spiders will spring from their perches after a flying insect and then float to the floor on a thin silk thread, still attached to the wall. They are really helpful in the house in controlling flies, gnats, and roaches. These little black spiders can bite but will only do so if mashed or picked up. The bite is something like a bee sting. The mother lays her eggs in a sac-like silk pouch, usually attached to the wall in a corner or under a windowsill. For an excellent observation lesson place an egg sac in a container to await hatching.

Acquisition and Handling

The cup and card method is the best way to capture one of these spiders. When the spider is on a flat surface, place the cup over him, and slide the card beneath the surface and the cup. You should not try to pick up the animal with your hand because, as I said, they can and will bite and they are so small that you might injure them.

Cage and Habitat Materials

The ventilated plastic shoe box or the 1-gallon large-mouth jar makes an excellent habitat for this spider (see illustrations in Fig. 5 and Fig. 6). Fill the container with a half-inch of aquarium gravel or potting soil substrate and decorate with small branches.

Temperature/Light/Humidity

These spiders do well at room temperature and available light. The humidity should not be allowed to cause condensation on the inside of the container. If this happens, simply open the lid and air it out.

Food and Water

Jumping spiders eat small insects that may be captured in your back porch insect trap as illustrated in Fig. 3. Another fun activity is to swat a fly, impale it on the end of a toothpick, and offer it to your captive. They should be fed one insect three or four times a week. They get their moisture from their food.

Maintenance

You should not keep these spiders in captivity long enough to have to clean anything. Do not leave live insects in the habitat overnight.

Release and Disposal

Believe it or not, these spiders are wonderful to have around the house. They are an excellent biological control for insect pests, so release the spider in any available houseplant. Take them outside if you don't dig spiders!

Notes and Afterthoughts

Your captive most likely will be a female, and if she builds a nest and lays her eggs, you might simply want to put the entire habitat outside and leave the top off.

Millipedes

Millipedes are not insects and they are not arachnids, and if
you are into counting legs, they are called diplopods. That
simply means they have two pairs of legs per segment of
their body. Down home, they call them thousand-leggers,
but they really only have 300 legs. Millipedes are found
under rocks in moist soil and leaf litter. They are nocturnal
animals. They defend themselves by discharging a strong-
smelling secretion that may be repellent and poisonous to
some animals. In spite of their defenses, millipedes are prey
to everything from spiders to birds.

Acquisition and Handling

If you have ever heard the phrase "leave no stone
unturned," turn a few over and you will find millipedes.
When you touch one, they immediately coil — which
makes them very easy to pick up. Those defense secretions
cannot be detected by the human nose but may cause
yellow stains on your fingers. They are not poisonous and
do not bite.

Cage and Habitat Materials

Wide-mouthed gallon jars and plastic shoe boxes are excellent temporary homes for these animals as illustrated in
Fig. 5 and Fig. 6. The preferable substrate would be moist
decaying leaf litter. You will never find them in daylight
unless you move your litter around.

Temperature/Lighting/Humidity

Millipedes can be maintained under standard lighting with
room temperature. They do, however, need high humidity,
so mist the substrate once a day. A good indication of
proper humidity would be condensation inside the
container.

Food and Water

Millipedes prefer decaying vegetation. You can supplement with spinach leaves, moist fruit such as peaches or plums, and an occasional smear of wet cat or dog food on a leaf. They get most of their water needs from the food. Feed small amounts every other day, and remove uneaten food at the end of each day.

Maintenance

Millipedes do best in unchanged environments. Replace substrate every two weeks unless the mold and fungus get nasty.

Release and Disposal

Release them as close to the place and time of the year as you collected them. If that should prove unfeasible, then release them in the same general area before the first frost.

Notes and Afterthoughts

Try not to trip them!

Scorpions

Scorpions are cousins of our more commonly recognized arachnids such as spiders and mites. They are arachnids because of their eight legs. Their peculiar body structure allows them quick movement. They have highly developed predatory instincts. While they may look like deadly animals, most species in the United States rarely grow more than two to three inches and are more afraid of you than the other way around. Some in Africa can reach as long as six to seven inches with considerable poison potential. They are secretive creatures that hide beneath rocks and logs most of the time. There is one species found in Arizona that has caused fatalities.

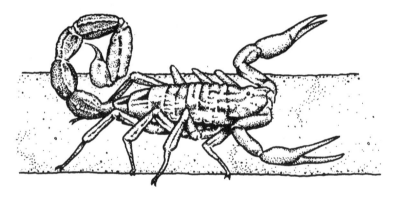

Acquisition and Handling

Turn over rocks, logs, or pieces of board to find scorpions. A scorpion may be lifted with a pair of forceps by grabbing the tail just behind the stinger. The safe way to catch them is to use a cup or small jar and an index card. Place the container over the animal and slide the card between the container and the ground.

Cage and Habitat Materials

A wide-mouth 1-gallon jar with holes in the lid makes the best cage for this creature. See the setup in Fig. 6. Do not put more than one scorpion in a jar. A 10-gallon aquarium can hold as many as four. Use a wire top for the aquarium not so much to prevent escape as to keep out little fingers.

Use about one inch of sand or aquarium gravel as substrate. Rocks and rotted logs will provide good cover. Do not use too much or you will never see your captive.

Temperature/Lighting/Humidity

Keep the scorpion at room temperature and away from direct sunlight. Do not allow the temperature to vary too much. The substrate needs to be kept relatively moist. Do not spray water directly on the animal because fungus infections could develop.

Food and Water

Feed your captive small insects such as roaches, crickets, and grasshoppers. Feed one insect about twice each week. Cut a piece of new sponge to fit a watch glass or jar lid and keep the sponge wet as shown in Fig. 17. When the scorpion is thirsty he will get his water from the sponge directly.

Maintenance

Remove uneaten insects and insect parts. Clean the water sponge frequently. Unless the habitat really gets nasty, it is best left alone.

Release and Disposal

Take the animal back where you found it. If that was the backyard, you might want to take him further out.

Notes and Afterthoughts

The sting from these animals is very painful. The best first aid I have used is a liberal application of a paste made from baking soda and water. You might also grab the sting, scream, and then jump up and down until the hurt goes away!

Tarantulas

Tarantulas are nocturnal creatures that actively hunt their prey. They live in holes in the ground which they line with silk. During the day they might be found under large flat rocks or pieces of wood. Tarantulas have multiple eyes and tactile leg hairs. The bite can be compared to that of a bee sting. It is best to keep a female as a pet as they live much longer than males, sometimes 25 years. A female can be recognized by the lack of claws on the palpi, the forwardmost appendages near the mouth.

Acquisition and Handling

The tarantula can be picked up by placing your index finger on the top of its body between the head and abdomen and pressing gently to the ground, then placing your thumb and middle finger on each side of the body at the base of the legs. Be gentle but firm. Another method of catching spiders and insects is to use a small jar or cup and an index card. Place the container over the animal and slip the card between the container and the ground.

Cage and Habitat Materials

An aquarium with a wire top, a plastic sweater box with air holes, or a large-mouth glass jar with holes in the lid make good, sound, escape-proof cages for tarantulas. These are shown in Fig. 21, Fig. 5, and Fig. 6. Sand or gravel may be placed in the container. Rocks may be stacked to form holes or caves. Stack carefully so they will not fall.

Temperature/Light/Humidity

Tarantulas do well at room temperature and any lighting except direct sunlight. If the habitat clouds with condensation, remove lid and allow to dry.

Food and Water

Feed two insects each week (crickets, grasshoppers, roaches, moths, etc.). Catch your crickets or grasshoppers from the woods, not from about the neighborhood. These insects store insecticide in their bodies and may be lethal to your tarantula. You can catch small flying insects by using the trap illustrated in Fig. 3. Provide water by cutting a sponge to fit inside a jar lid and keep the sponge wet. See illustration in Fig. 17. Do not drop water directly on the tarantula because this may cause a fungus to develop.

Maintenance

Do not overfeed. Remove remaining insect parts and waste material daily. Clean the water sponge regularly and change every two weeks.

Release and Disposal

Try to release the animal near the time and place it was captured. If that is not possible, release in an open field as far from the roadway as possible.

Notes and Afterthoughts

Our tarantulas are not really tarantulas. That name belongs to a group of European spiders. They are actually hairy megalomorphs. That doesn't cause as much commotion as saying tarantula.

Wolf Spiders

Wolf spiders are very common "sidewalk" spiders. They are large, four to six inches across, and have voracious appetites. Their predatory nature is where they get their name. They do not spin a web but hide under debris.

Acquisition and Handling

Wolf spiders are quick and agile and catching one is reserved for people under ten years old! The best method is to use a cup or wide-mouth jar and a piece of cardboard such as an index card. Trap the spider beneath the cup and slide the cardboard between the ground and the mouth of the jar. Don't try to pick them up because there is not enough body to grab. They may be found roaming across the top of leaves, piles of forest debris, and at times, crossing the sidewalk in the front yard.

A trick I use is, with a garden hose, spray the cracks in the ground around the foundation of the house and when the cracks fill with water the spiders will surface.

Cage and Habitat Materials

An aquarium with a wire top, a plastic sweater box with air holes, or a large-mouth glass jar with holes in the lid make good, sound, escape-proof cages for wolf spiders. One inch of sand or small gravel will make a good substrate. They require a hiding place and I would suggest you use a piece of curved bark. You may use flat stones stacked up to form a cave but be sure to stack them carefully and avoid moving the habitat so they won't fall and squash your captive.

Temperature/Light/Humidity

The wolf spider does well at room temperature and any lighting except direct sunlight. If the habitat clouds with condensation, remove lid or top and allow to dry.

Food and Water

Feed two live insects each week. These can be crickets, grasshoppers, roaches, moths, and others. You can catch insects by using the insect trap shown in Fig. 3. Use only flying insects or insects from the woods and fields and not from about the neighborhood. The local ground dwelling insects store insecticides and that will do in your pet. Provide water by cutting a sponge to fit inside a jar lid and keep the sponge wet. See illustration, Fig. 17.

Maintenance

Do not overfeed as the extra insects might attack your spider. Remove remaining insect parts and waste material daily. Clean the water sponge regularly and change every two weeks.

Release and Disposal

Try to release the animal near the time and place he was captured. If that is not possible release in an open area as far from the roadway as feasible.

Notes and Afterthoughts

Use a new sponge for the water. Wolf spiders don't tolerate Pine-Sol real well!

Chapter 3
ARTHROPODS

Invertebrate organisms of the phylum
Arthropoda, having a horny, segmented
external coverings and jointed limbs.

Ants (Red or Black Harvest Ants)

Ants are industrious creatures and highly social. They will construct very intricate mazes of tunnels in an artificial environment. The ants you use will most likely be workers, which are all females. Most of them will die within six or eight weeks without the presence of a queen. During that time they will build an impressive "city," but you must care for them properly.

Acquisition and Handling

You can use ants from the park or your backyard. Stay away from fire ants because they seem to escape from just about anywhere. You can catch an ant by allowing it to crawl onto a stick or pencil and then simply shaking it into your habitat.

Check with your local hobby shop or pet store and you can order ants through the mail. The ants you catch or buy will be female workers who are really responsible for the observable construction. Needless to say, they all will sting you! As a child I really disliked being stung by anything. The pain was not so bad, I just did not like the first aid. My grandmother was convinced that tobacco "drew the poison out!" She dipped snuff, try to imagine! Be aware of allergies to insect venom. The pain and swelling may be relieved by applying cold compresses or a paste made from baking soda and water. I prefer just jumping up and down and hollering for about five minutes and it goes away.

Cage and Habitat Materials

The easiest and safest way to house an ant is to buy a ready-made ant farm. If you are a carpenter at heart, go to a hobby shop or pet shop, look at one, then go home and build it. The substrate should be construction sand or sandy loam. I have included an illustration of what is available in Fig. 19.

Fill this habitat half with sand and add about two ounces of water. It is best to use distilled water.

Temperature/Light/Humidity

Never leave the habitat in direct sunlight. Don't take it in- and outdoors. Temperature changes are not tolerated. You must add a few drops of water every other day but be careful not to saturate the sand. Available light will suffice.

Food and Water

Ants eat almost anything. But remember, they are tiny creatures and they eat tiny meals. About half a corn flake is enough food for the entire colony for a week. You can feed them a few bread crumbs soaked in sugar water or honey. They eat leaves, especially fruit tree leaves.

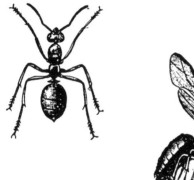

Maintenance

Remove uneaten food at the end of the day. Don't worry about the ants that die as they will become dinner for the others.

Release and Disposal

If you caught them in the yard or park, put them back. If you ordered them through the mail and they are harvester ants, you can still let them go outside. Release is really not a concern because after a period of time there are fewer and fewer and then there are none!

Notes and Afterthoughts

The main cause of death among captured ant colonies is overfeeding; be careful. Don't mix ants from different colonies; they will fight to the death.

Ant Lions (Doodle Bugs)

The ant lion is the larval form of a group of nondescript dragonfly or lace-wing looking insects. It gets its name from its habit of trapping its prey in a funnel-shaped depression in the sand. These sand traps can be located in just about any dry, protected, sandy area where the weather will not destroy it. The larvae has a short, thick, fleshy body with disproportionately large caliper-like jaws that grasp its prey.

Acquisition and Handling

You'll find them in soft sand, and it is a simple matter to use a cup and scoop up the sand and the ant lion in one scoop. They don't bite but you may squash them trying to pick them up, so the scoop is the best way.

Cage and Habitat Materials

Fill a shallow pan with about two inches of fine sand. The sides of the pan should extend about one inch above the sand surface. Add ant lions about one per five square inches of sand surface.

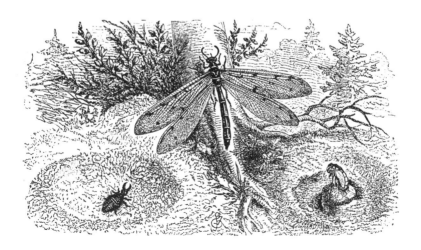

Food and Water

Feed them live ants or stunned flies. There must be some movement in the food items. You can trick them by dropping a dead fly in the sand funnel, then using a thin wire to "tickle" the fly until the ant lion grabs it. One food item about three times a week is a good maintenance diet.

Release and Disposal

Try to release the ant lions where and when you collected them. Not much is known about the time period of their life cycle, but it is between one and three years.

Notes and Afterthoughts

They travel backwards everywhere they go! Some people tell me I do that.

Bessbugs
(Short-Horned Stag Beetles)

These bugs are black and shiny, somewhat flattened, and they have enormous jaws. They inhabit decaying logs and stumps. The larval form is a long, yellow, segmented worm. They are also sometimes called patent-leather beetles.

Acquisition and Handling

These beetles are easily picked up with thumb and fore-finger on each side of their bodies. You can find them in rotted logs or stumps by breaking the wood apart or some-times just by turning it over. Take care not to get too close to those jaws as they can deliver quite a pinch.

Cage and Habitat Materials

Choose a container to fit your space! The substrate should be damp leaves; then you should supply a good amount of

moist, decaying wood. A 10-gallon aquarium suits this purpose and will house five to ten beetles.

Temperature/Light/Humidity

Room temperature and light is sufficient; they prefer high humidity, and this can be accomplished by daily misting of the decaying wood and leaves. A plant atomizer is good for this purpose.

Food and Water

The high humidity will be sufficient water, and they will happily munch on the decaying wood which you can replace and renew as needed.

Maintenance

Do not allow the wood or leaves to grow fungus, as this may lead to bacterial buildup and death of your captive.

Release and Disposal

Put him back where you found him!

Notes and Afterthoughts

These are not long-term captives, one reason being they don't live that long!

Butterflies (Painted Lady)

The painted lady butterfly is found throughout the world. It is a fairly common species, and at times, hundreds can be seen migrating across the country. After hatching from a small pale green egg, the larva pulls the edges of a leaf together and begins feeding within. After several months (usually five), the larva hangs upside down and prepares to pupate. At this time, the larva is developing into a chrysalis or pupa. After 24 hours the caterpillar's skin splits and the chrysalis wiggles free and, in about four hours, hardens. The adult emerges in seven to ten days. The process from egg to larva, from chrysalis to adult, is called complete metamorphosis and occurs in other flying insects, such as moths, flies, wasps, and bees.

Acquisition and Handling

Butterfly larvae can be purchased through any biological supply company and will be shipped in a plastic vial with tissue paper inside the lid. Contact your local college science department for supply information. Do not handle the butterfly for any reason.

Cage and Habitat Material

Place the vial in a well-lit area away from direct sunlight where the temperature remains between 70 and 80 degrees Fahrenheit. In five to ten days the larvae will crawl to the top of the vial and hang from the filter paper. After the chrysalis has developed (in one or two days), place the filter paper with the insects attached in a sweater or shoe storage box (see illustration, Fig. 5). The butterflies should emerge seven to ten days later. Place small potted plants in the box, and in about a week the butterflies will deposit eggs on the plants. The eggs will hatch in three to five days and can be transferred to fresh medium. Additional prepared medium may be purchased along with the larvae.

Food and Water

Fill an insect waterer (Fig. 1) with a 5 percent sugar solution (1 teaspoon sugar to 1/3 cup water) on which the butterflies will feed. The food supply for the larvae will come with your order from the supply company.

Maintenance

Depending upon the length of their stay, the cleaning of the habitat should be kept to a minimum. As the butterflies emerge from their chrysalis, the filter paper can be changed and the box wiped out with a wet sponge. Do not use any kind of soap. Refill the waterer as needed.

Release and Disposal

When your colony has served its purpose, ask around if any one else wants to experience the wonders of butterfly development. Call your local nature center, elementary school, or the biology department of a college. You can just take your butterflies out on a warm summer day and turn them loose. They are free you know!

Notes and Afterthoughts

If you find a cocoon of some type, it will develop in a similar manner. When the insect emerges and dries, let him go!

Caterpillars

Ah the caterpillar, a marvelous little eating machine! The caterpillar is the larval stage of the complete metamorphosis of some insects. They pass through four distinct growing stages — the egg, larva, pupa, and adult. The caterpillar is the active feeding stage, while the pupa is the inactive resting stage during which the larva changes into the adult. If fed properly, the caterpillar can transform before your very eyes!

Acquisition and Handling

You will usually find caterpillars crawling across the sidewalk or munching leaves out in the bushes by the porch. Do not touch an unidentified caterpillar as some of them possess poisonous spines. Use an open-top container and a small stick to flip them inside.

Cage and Habitat Materials

The plastic sweater or shoe box as shown in Fig. 5 makes a good brooder for caterpillars. Place several layers of newsprint or paper towel on the bottom. Branches and twigs should be added for crawling space and point of attachment when the pupa is formed.

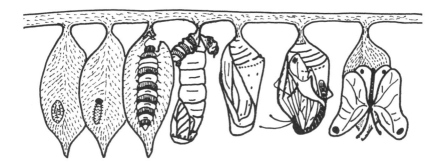

Temperature/Light/Humidity

Place the container near a window for heat and light. Avoid direct sunlight. The humidity will be provided by the greenery in the cage.

Food and Water

It is best to find the caterpillar on a plant — that will tell you what to feed him. If he is on the sidewalk, it will be necessary to look him up in a book and find out what he eats. Keep a fresh batch of greenery available at all times. He will get his moisture from the plants. The length of time he eats before forming the pupa will depend on his species.

Maintenance

Replace greenery daily.

Release and Disposal

After the new insect has dried and his wings are fully extended, take him outside and let him go. You will be lucky if you get to see him emerge. Check often!

Notes and Afterthoughts

The terms pupa, cocoon, and chrysalis all refer to the same stage of development when you are reading about caterpillars.

Cicadas

The cicada, which is incorrectly called a locust, is common throughout eastern and central North America. There are some ten thousand species worldwide, so we won't worry a lot about those. Our local cicadas are known according to their time of development in the ground. We have 1-, 3-, 13-, and 17-year cicadas. The females lay their eggs in a crack in a branch whereupon the eggs hatch and fall to the ground. The larvae burrow down to the minute roots of various trees and there they develop for whatever period of time their species dictate. When the time is right, the larvae will climb out onto a tree trunk or any upright surface and shed its exoskeleton. The adult emerges and the male flies to the most convenient perch and begins screaming. This ear-piercing scream can be heard throughout the warm summer months. The noise is definitely to attract females. After mating, everybody involved dies!

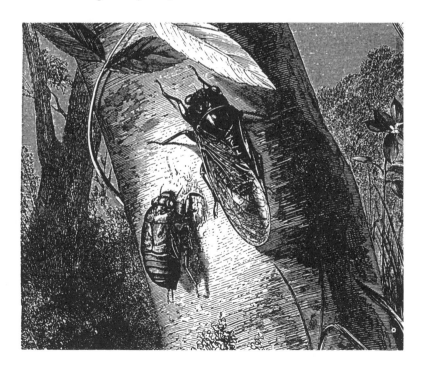

Acquisition and Handling

If you are under the age of ten, grabbing a cicada is no problem. If you are above that age, any dime-store insect net or fish net will work fine. It may be necessary to attach these nets with tape to the longest pole you can find. They may be picked up and handled just about any way if you are not susceptible to the creeps!

Cage and Habitat Materials

A wire cage of any gauge smaller than the cicada will work just fine. You can also use the trusty old 10-gallon aquarium with a wire top. Branches should be added to allow the cicada a place to perch. The cage should be mobile as you will want to move it when the screaming starts.

Temperature/Light/Humidity

Cicadas may be maintained at room temperature, light, and humidity.

Food and Water

The adult stage of the cicada is not known to eat or drink!

Maintenance

No maintenance required.

Release and Disposal

Cicadas are interesting to watch and listen to but only live two to four weeks in the adult stage, so you should release them back into the trees as soon as possible. Only mass concentrations of these creatures pose any threat to the trees in your yard.

Notes and Afterthoughts

The cicada does have a long, siphon-like proboscis (nose) but it doesn't sting; it really doesn't do much of anything!

Cockroaches

There are a number of different species of cockroaches that live with and among us all the time. Why would you want to raise cockroaches? You shouldn't tell anybody or they'll think you're weird! Really, they are interesting to watch, easy to raise, and if you keep other insect-eating creatures, they are a wonderful food item. For observation purposes, you should obtain one of the larger species, such as the Blaberus from South America or the hissing cockroach from Africa. These tropical varieties cannot survive a freeze, therefore you should not worry about escapees.

Most of the germs carried by cockroaches are picked up in their not-too-clean natural habitat and then transported to human-used surfaces. If a cockroach is raised in a clean environment, you will produce a "clean" cockroach. Explain to your student the difference between the two and rest assured that you won't come down with something.

Acquisition and Handling

The exotic breeds may be obtained from any biological supply company. You may contact your local school biology teacher or local zoo reptile department and find a source. Cockroaches don't bite although some have sharp spines at the edges of their body that will stick you if you grasp too firmly. I find it easier to let the cockroach crawl on your hand as opposed to trying to grab anything.

Cage and Habitat Materials

The plastic shoe box (see illustration in Fig. 5) will do nicely as a cage. The top should be secured with a rubber band around each end of the entire box. Fill the shoe box with one inch of cereal flakes such as bran or corn. "Der-ders" may be added as hiding places. Now you're wondering what a "der-der" is. Cardboard toilet paper rolls or paper towel rolls are called "der-ders." Put one up to your mouth and the sound that comes out is something like "der-da-der-dot-der-der!" Try it!

Temperature/Light/Humidity

Roaches can survive a wide range of temperature, and room temperature is adequate. Room light and normal humidity suffice. The warmer they are the more activity there will be.

Food and Water

Cockroaches will eat anything, even the glue in book bindings. I feed mine a smear of soft cat or dog food on a piece of paper. A weekly slice of apple or potato is nourishing and provides sufficient moisture. Just to be safe, include an insect waterer as seen in Fig. 1. They should be fed at least twice a week.

Maintenance

Remove uneaten food at the end of the day and dismantle and thoroughly clean the habitat once each week. While

you're cleaning, you can dump the roaches (cereal and all) into a glass container (they can't crawl up glass). Use only warm water and a plastic scouring pad to clean.

Release and Disposal

Call your school's science department or the local nature center — perhaps they need your collection! If not, place the roaches (cereal and all) in a sealed plastic bag and place them in the freezer. That's really the humane way to do it!

Notes and Afterthoughts

Fortunately for us, cross-breeding exotic breeds with our local species is not possible. Even so, don't release these creatures in the woods.

Crickets

Crickets are useful for classroom or science projects in such areas as development, insect sounds, and for food for other animals. They can be raised year round with a minimum of equipment. They are easy to get and easy to get rid of.

Acquisition and Handling

During the spring and summer, crickets may be found just about anywhere. The place I look first is along the foundation of my house after dark. If they aren't crawling up the wall, just fill the cracks between the foundation and the dirt with water and they will come out. You might also try under the dog house. If you don't hunt, call your local zoo reptile department about their cricket supply.

Catching a cricket is just a matter of a quick grab. If you hold them too long or squeeze too hard, they will bite. I put the cardboard from toilet paper in the cage (with one end stapled closed) and the crickets hide inside making it easy to transfer them.

Cage and Habitat Materials

Depending upon the number of crickets you require, the cages will vary. I use a 30-gallon metal trash can. It requires no top and little maintenance. You may use any aquarium with a wide top. A dry sand substrate about one inch deep, cardboard containers, egg cartons, or cardboard toilet paper rolls make good hiding places.

Temperature/Light/Humidity

These factors determine how fast your crickets develop and how long they live. Nymphs (newborn) kept at 82 degrees Fahrenheit will mature in 30 to 35 days. A few degrees lower and it may take twice as long. The adult lives for about 90 days.

A clamp-on light with a low-wattage bulb will provide heat. Breeding is facilitated by moistening the sand. I discuss breeding in the last paragraph of this section. Otherwise, moisture can be provided by adding sliced apple or potato.

Food and Water

Crickets will eat just about anything that doesn't eat them first. Provide them with oatmeal, bran flakes, leafy veggies, cornmeal, sliced apples, sliced potatoes, or dry dog and cat food. Feed about every other day.

For water, cut a new sponge to fit a large jar lid and keep it moist. Another method that is a little harder to clean is a chick waterer, shown in Fig. 13. Fill the water trough with aquarium gravel and it will stay wet. Crickets will drown themselves in open water.

Release and Disposal

Crickets are hazardous to the health of your houseplants and landscape in general. So, depending upon the age of your children and politics of your situation, you will most likely opt for taking them out in the country and releasing them.

Notes and Afterthoughts

Don't overcrowd crickets; they are cannibals. Keep about 500 for each 10-gallon container size.

Crickets will lay their eggs in moist sand. The eggs are small, banana-shaped, yellowish white objects. They are laid singly, not in clusters. The eggs will hatch in two or three weeks.

Female crickets are easily distinguished from males by a long needlelike ovipositor (egg layer) at the end of their tails. Sometimes the crickets will eat the eggs. Place a piece of screen wire over a dish of moist sand. The screen mesh should be large enough for the ovipositor to pass through but small enough to prevent the adults from eating the eggs.

CAUTION: Do not feed wild-caught crickets to your other animals. They might contain stored insecticides.

Earwigs

It's 3 a.m. and time for a trip to the kitchen for some water. On comes the light and there scurrying across the floor is a small black bug with scissors on its back end. This fearsome looking creature is the common earwig. There are some 900 species throughout the world. Earwigs spend the day hidden away in dry, upright crevices. At night they search for food. In late March they lay 20 to 80 small curly white eggs. The female stays with her eggs during their three- to four-week incubation period. During this time she is more likely to attack an intruder by biting with her mouth and pinching with her scissors. They are not venomous.

Acquisition and Handling

If you don't have a population in your house, you can find earwigs outside hidden away in dry, usually upright crevices and under loose bark on rotting trees. Common earwigs are also found tucked away on the petals of dahlias. The easiest way to pick them up is to herd them into a paper cup with a twig. They can bite, but it usually does not break the skin.

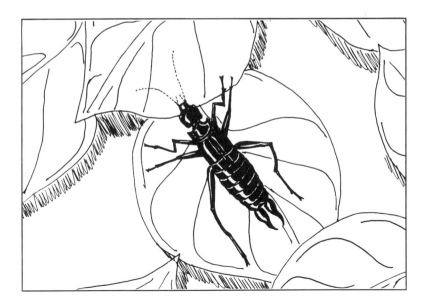

Cage and Habitat Materials

A large-mouthed gallon jar, as shown in Fig. 6, containing one or two inches of potting soil and a small piece of bark for hiding makes a good earwig habitat.

Temperature/Light/Humidity

Room temperature, light, and humidity are usually sufficient for maintaining earwigs. You might want to add a bit of moisture to the potting soil occasionally by misting with a plant atomizer.

Food and Water

Their diets include both plant and animal material. They will eat fruit, leaves, and flowers. They also seem to like small insects such as moths and small crickets. Use the insect trap as shown in Fig. 3 to catch the moths. Be careful not to add too many insects, or they might eat your earwig. Feed one or two food items about every third day.

Maintenance

Clean and change habitat if a fungal or bacterial growth appears in the soil. Otherwise, it is best to leave it alone.

Release and Disposal

Contact teachers, both grade school and college, when your earwig collection needs a home. They can cause plant damage, and it may be best to put the collection into a plastic bag and let them spend the night in a freezer. I can live with that method more easily than dunking them in a jar of rubbing alcohol and watching them do the backstroke!

Notes and Afterthoughts

They only live about one year, and if you keep them that long, you are amazing!

Grasshoppers

The big, scary, yellow grasshopper that is heard and seen throughout most of North America is called the differential grasshopper. They grow to three inches long and eat anything associated with plants. They breed readily in captivity and exhibit an incomplete metamorphosis; that is, the babies look like small versions of the adults and are called nymphs.

Acquisition and Handling

Anyone under ten years of age can catch a grasshopper without even thinking about it. Techniques will vary according to experience. They will bite if squeezed. An insect net may be used for those who don't care to grab! They are easily picked up by grasping the jumping legs with thumb and forefinger. They may be found in tall grass during any part of the summer.

Cage and Habitat Materials

The 10-gallon aquarium with screen wire top as shown in Fig. 9 is an excellent habitat for grasshoppers. The substrate should be one to two inches of either sand or topsoil.

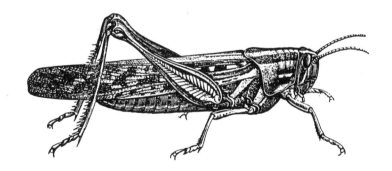

Branches can be added for decoration and to make observation easier.

Temperature/Light/Humidity

The warmer the grasshopper, the more active he will be. They can survive with room lighting and room humidity.

Food and Water

Grasshoppers will eat any form of plant, i.e., leaves, fruits, flowers, live or dead, fresh or rotting! They get the water they need from their food. Add fresh greenery daily and remove the old stuff.

Maintenance

The entire habitat should be dismantled and cleaned once a week. Use a mild dishwashing detergent to clean and rinse thoroughly.

Release and Disposal

Grasshoppers cause a lot of damage to everything, so you might be doing your bit for conservation if you put your grasshopper in a nice cloth or plastic bag and slip him into the freezer for a couple of hours! If that's not your bag, just take him out the back door and wave bye-bye!

Notes and Afterthoughts

There are many different kinds of grasshoppers but they can all be maintained in much the same way.

June Beetles

These brown marbles with wings are also called June bugs or Japanese beetles. June beetles are usually abducted during their annual summer meetings on the back porch! They hover like small, brown helicopters rising slowly from the concrete surface, then dash headlong into the wall! By this time, they have fulfilled their purpose in life, that is, to mate and now they simply wait to die. Banging into the wall seems to bring immediacy to that process!

Acquisition and Handling

The quick-grab method works every time! Or your child may want to keep the one that followed him into the kitchen! They don't bite and can be handled safely.

Cage and Habitat Materials

Any closed-in container will do for this temporary resident. The 1-gallon jar with lid is the most easily handled and keeps the insect most visible. Add one to two inches of gravel, sand, or soil and you can decorate with twigs as you so desire. Furniture is not really a necessity here.

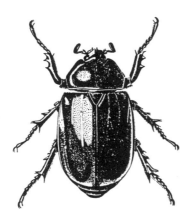

Temperature/Light/Humidity

Room temperature, light, and humidity will be sufficient for this insect.

Food and Water

Water may be supplied by misting the inside of the container slightly each day. In the adult stages, June bugs are not big eaters, but will suck juices from soft leaves such as spinach, lettuce, carrot tops, and other greens.

Maintenance

Remove any decayed leaf material or moldy substrate frequently. Do not be concerned, but your captive most likely won't live long anyway.

Release and Disposal

Worry about something else! Or, you can place your bugs in a plastic bag and put them in the freezer for a few hours.

Notes and Afterthoughts

If you have other pets, don't feed the dead June bugs to them because June beetles harbor residuals from pesticides. The larvae form of the June beetle is the grub worm, and if you value your lawn, you might not be too concerned with the June beetle's conservation!

Katydids

The katydid is a type of grasshopper that represents the ultimate in camouflage techniques. When sitting in its natural habitat in trees and bushes, it is almost invisible as it looks exactly like a folded leaf. Its odd shape and slow, deliberate movements make it a very interesting captive for observation.

Acquisition and Handling

The katydid is most often brought in from the back porch where they seem to land frequently during the summer months. They may be picked up using the thumb and forefinger at the knees of their jumping legs and wings at the same time. They will bite, so one must be careful about squeezing. They may be collected in the fields on upright long-bladed grass and low bushes.

Cage and Habitat Materials

The 10-gallon aquarium with screen wire top is an excellent habitat for the katydid. This setup is illustrated in Fig. 9. The substrate should be two inches of either sand or topsoil. Branches can be added for decoration and to make observation easier.

Temperature/Light/Humidity

Katydids prefer warm, moist habitats. The warmer it is the more active they will be. They can survive with room lighting, and humidity can be provided with a wide, shallow water dish.

Food and Water

Katydids will eat almost any type of plant, i.e., leaves or flowers, both live or dead. They get the water they need from their food. The shallow, wide water dish provides humidity for the habitat.

Maintenance

Katydids should be fed once each day, and all uneaten food should be removed at the end of the day. The entire habitat should be dismantled and cleaned once each week. Use a mild dishwashing liquid to clean and rinse thoroughly.

Release and Disposal

Simply carry Katy back out to the woods and fields and wave bye-bye! This should be done before the cool weather of the fall sets in.

Notes and Afterthoughts

A good rule of thumb: one animal per habitat. There are, of course, many many different kinds of grasshoppers, but they can all be maintained in much the same way.

Ladybugs

Ladybugs are small beetles with a round body shaped like half a pea. They are often bright red or yellow with intermittent red, white or yellow spots. Ladybugs feed chiefly on plant lice and aphids. For this reason fruit growers find ladybugs very helpful. The lifespan of the ladybug is about one year. The eggs are laid in the spring and develop into darkish grey larvae with orange spots. These soft-bodied, carrot-shaped larvae appear quite unlike the round, hardbodied adults. Both forms have a voracious appetite, and it has been claimed that one beetle is capable of eating more than 50 aphids a day when they're actively feeding. The pupa of the ladybug does not spin a cocoon. It attaches to a leaf by cementing its abdomen to the leaf. The new adult beetles appear during the first week of June. They are active crawlers and fliers and will move around nearly five miles in as little as three days. Throughout the summer and autumn the adults are abundant in the city parks and flower gardens. As winter approaches they migrate to the mountains where they congregate in large numbers prior to winter hibernation. While in this hibernation form the adults do not feed but live off stored fat.

Acquisition and Handling

Ladybugs are easily captured by placing the open mouth of a prescription medicine bottle or test tube near them as they perch on a branch and simply flipping them into the vial with a twig. They are really too small to pick up with your fingers without causing them harm. It is best to simply move them from place to place with a stick. Take care here as they are excellent fliers.

Cage and Habitat Materials

Ladybugs can easily be placed in a plastic shoe box as illustrated in Fig. 5, or a gallon jar container as illustrated in Fig. 6. Habitat materials may be those branches on which the insect was found.

Temperature/Light/Humidity

Room temperature is sufficient. Try to avoid extremes in temperature such as near an air conditioning vent or in the bright sun of a window. Room lighting and humidity will do.

Food and Water

Keep for only a short period of time, providing them with a wick type waterer as illustrated in Fig. 1. Use a mixture of one teaspoon sugar to 1/2 cup water. Beetles kept during the summer must be fed aphids. Check the underside of the leaves in the area where you found the ladybug. You may also order aphids from a biological supply house and you can get that information from your local biology teacher. About one aphid a day will keep your ladybug healthy.

Maintenance

For the period of time they are in captivity no maintenance is required. The beetles store fat during the summer feeding so they can survive during the winter cold.

Release/Disposal

Return to the place where you found the beetle and it can return to controlling plant lice and insects. They live about one year.

Mealworms

Mealworms are an interesting project in more ways than one. They can be easily raised as food for other small animals such as lizards, frogs, toads, tarantulas, and scorpions. The larval stage that you purchase at the pet shop can be easily cultured and you may want to observe the four distinct stages that you will find in these insects. The larvae will eat and grow depending upon the temperature and food availability. They will pupate and the adults will emerge two to three weeks after pupation. The adults will begin to lay eggs seven to ten days later and the eggs will hatch fourteen days later. This entire cycle is interesting and is a good topic for various science projects.

Acquisition and Handling

Mealworm larvae may be purchased at almost any pet shop or may be ordered in bulk from a number of biological supply companies. None of the stages of the mealworm are capable of biting and they may simply be handled with fingers.

Cage and Habitat Materials

The wide-mouthed gallon jar or a plastic sweater or shoe box make excellent habitats for mealworms as shown in the

illustrations in Fig. 5 and Fig. 6. The gallon jar should be covered with cotton gauze and secured with a rubber band. The plastic box lids can be aerated by heating a paper clip held with pliers over an open flame and then quickly melting holes in the lid and sides of the plastic box. Mealworms live in their own food; oatmeal is the best choice but crushed breakfast cereal or bran meal would be suitable. Fill the habitat one-half to three-quarters full; place shredded paper on top of the cereal. This habitat will hold fifty to seventy-five worms.

Temperature/Light/Humidity

They do best in indirect light at room temperature (70 to 75 degrees Fahrenheit). Humidity is supplied with the water source — a slice or two of apple or potato.

Food and Water

As already stated, the mealworm lives in its own food. Therefore, it will only be necessary to replace the food when the cereal has been eaten away or becomes powdery. Water for the growing insects is supplied by a slice of apple or a few potato pieces which should be replaced about every three days.

Maintenance

Renew the substrate about once each month. Do not allow substrate to mold or rot.

Release and Disposal

Your culture of mealworms will be gladly accepted by anyone who has small reptiles, amphibians, or birds. As a last resort give them to the pet shop.

Notes and Afterthoughts

The entire culture may be held dormant by placing it in a cloth bag with some shredded newspaper and then placing the whole thing in the refrigerator. This will keep the worms alive for over a month with no care at all.

Praying Mantises

Everyone has had a glimpse of these delicate creatures whose name describes their seemingly prayerful attitude. With heads shaped like Napoleon's hat and eyes on each corner of their heads, they seem to watch your every move. They have the ability to change colors to blend in with their surroundings which is necessary for hiding from predators and for catching their food. They are slow moving and do not hunt for food. Instead, they wait patiently for their prey, usually insects, to stray within reach and grasp them with their forelegs. The mantises have wings and are good fliers but do not fly off unless really pressured.

During mating, the females are likely to consume the males as just another meal. The females lay 80 to 100 eggs in a tough spongy sack which they attach to a tree. The young hatch together and at first hang from the egg capsule by silken threads which are manufactured from the abdomen. They grow in gradual stages multiplying in size up to twelve times before becoming an adult.

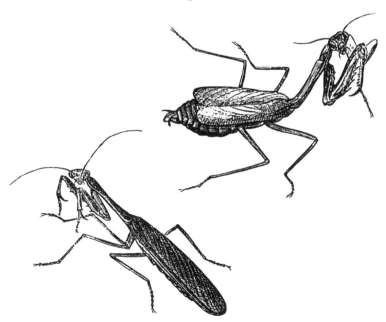

Acquisition and Handling

It is best not to try to pick up a praying mantis; they are very fragile and skittish. They can be coaxed into a coffee can by using a small twig to guide them in.

Cage and Habitat Materials

An appropriate container is a gallon jar as illustrated in Fig. 6. Insert a small branch for climbing. Aquarium gravel, sand, or clean soil makes an excellent substrate.

Temperature/Lighting/Humidity

Avoid extremes in temperature; room temperature should do well. Do not place the habitat in direct sunlight for long periods of time. Room humidity will suffice.

Food and Water

Feed any kind of living insects — crickets, ants, grasshoppers, or flies. Feed one to five insects daily using forceps to hold the insects close enough for it to capture. The insects must be moving to attract the mantis' attention. Spray the cage daily with water as the mantis will drink from droplets of water on twigs. You may catch small flying insects by using the trap shown in Fig. 3.

Maintenance

The entire habitat should be changed once a week and uneaten insects removed daily.

Release and Disposal

Let the mantis go at the point where you found him. Release him during the warm months.

Notes and Afterthoughts

The mantises are cannibalistic; keep only one per cage. The average life span is one year.

Pussmoth Larvae or Asps

All furry critters are not necessarily warm and cuddly. During the fall months you may encounter a small furry caterpillar camouflaged in the leaves or crawling up your garage door. Asps are the larval form of the pussmoth which is a light colored moth about one inch long which you can see around your porch light in May and June. Reddish-brown eggs are laid on the upper surfaces of leaves of poplar and willow trees and are hatched in June. The caterpillars eat leaves throughout July, August, and September. Then a cocoon is formed in a crevice of the bark of a tree where they remain over winter and from which the moth emerges in the spring.

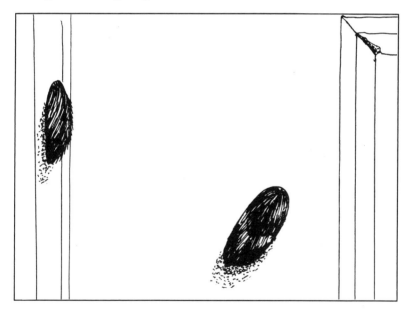

The only time this critter is dangerous is in the caterpillar form. When contact is made with the hair on its back, an acid solution is secreted from glands in the chest region onto the hairs. If you have ever been stung by an asp, you know why it is important to be able to recognize it and thus be able to avoid it. Capturing an asp could be beneficial, particularly in a classroom setting, to teach children and adults to be able to distinguish it from other harmless caterpillars.

Acquisition and Handling

Use a stick and flip him into a jar. Handling is not a question — don't!

Cage and Habitat Materials

Punch small air holes in a jar lid. Fill jar with a half inch of dead and decayed leaves. Add a stem or branch for climbing.

Temperature/Light/Humidity

Keep them in a cool part of the room in normal room lighting. Sprinkle the leaves with water when they appear dry.

Food and Water

Feed a small slice of apple or potato about once each week. They will get their water from the moist leaves and their food.

Maintenance

Condensation on the sides of the jar means that you have added too much water. Just open the lid and allow it to air out for a few minutes. You are only going to keep it for a short time so maintenance is not a concern.

Release and Disposal

To release or not to release is the question. If you have all the convictions of a monk, take these caterpillars far into the woods and dump them at the base of a tree.

Notes and Afterthoughts

Caution: do not keep these for too long. Store the habitat in a safe place when you are not directly supervising observations.

Silkworms

Silkworms do just what you think they do — they produce silk. The young caterpillar of the silkworm moth produces all of the natural silk in the world. It has been so thoroughly domesticated that it can no longer live in the wild.

Acquisition and Handling

You may purchase silkworms or their eggs from any biological supply house. Contact your local college biology department for sources. None of the growth stages should be handled as they are very fragile.

Cage and Habitat Materials

Clean out a shoe box or gallon milk carton that has been cut to about eight inches deep. It does not need a cover. This will hold about 25 caterpillars. The stems of the mulberry leaves will provide a resting place for the adult moths.

Temperature/Lighting/Humidity

Room light, temperature, and humidity will do well.

Food and Water

Silkworms feed exclusively on mulberry leaves. Add a fresh supply every day to keep them happy. Lettuce can be substituted for the leaves but only for a very short time. Mulberry leaves may be kept fresh in the refrigerator for several days.

Maintenance

Keep the container clean by recycling the mulberry leaves every day. Do this by allowing the caterpillars to climb onto the new leaves and removing the old leaves at the stem. Dump the container out to clean the old leaves and castings. Do not handle the caterpillars unless necessary because they easily develop infections.

Release and Disposal

Call your school and ask some teachers if they want the colony. Teachers, ask your students if they want to take on a neat project. It would do well if they had a lot of mulberry trees.

Notes and Afterthoughts

The caterpillar will live about 30 days munching on leaves and growing from 1/8th inch to 3 1/5 inches. They pass through several moltings as they grow larger, and you will find the exoskeletons in the container. Toward the end of their growth and life they will spin a silken cocoon. Put twigs in a cross-hatched pattern in the box to which they can attach the cocoons. A cream-colored moth will emerge at the end of 10 days. It cannot fly and therefore may be kept in the same container. The female lays her eggs on the bottom of the container within 48 hours. Eggs which have been fertilized will turn dark but the unfertilized ones will remain cream colored. The adult moths will die within a week. The eggs will hatch in a week, and the cycle begins again. Eggs can be stored in the refrigerator during the winter and cultured when the leaf supply is available.

If you want to use the silk, you must boil the cocoon before the moth begins to emerge. The boiling kills the moth and removes the glue holding the silken thread together. The single thread over a half-mile long can be wound around a smooth stick.

Chapter 4
BIRDS

Members of the class Aves, which includes warm-blooded, egg-laying feathered vertebrates with forelimbs modified to form wings.

93

Chickens

If you have ever visited a state fair you will know that chickens come in all shapes, sizes, and colors. The smaller of the chickens is called the bantee. It is a high-strung little bird. It doesn't require much space but requires constant care. The larger chickens, such as the white leghorn, are usually the ones that come to us as pets. Chickens are restricted in residential areas because of their space requirements and the noise they make.

Acquisition and Handling

Unfortunately, most pet chickens come through the pet trade in the form of a gift for Easter. Most chickens obtained this way are cockerels and usually of the lesser meat producing breeds. Other sources of chickens might be a simple purchase at the feed store, or they may be ordered through the mail from hatcheries. In some cases they are simply the result of a successful lesson with a home incubator. Newly hatched chickens should not be handled much as they are quite delicate. The youngsters are also prone to jumping out of one's hand, so they should be cradled firmly but gently. The adults look fierce but can just be grabbed and held onto.

Cage and Habitat Materials

For the period of time that you wish to keep a chicken as a pet, simple arrangements are best. For young chicks, a 20-gallon aquarium or larger may be set up. I use multi-layers of newsprint because of its ease in changing and its absorbency. For chicks one day to ten days old, it is necessary to set up a brood light which will be a low-wattage bulb in a reflector globe placed at one end of the cage. See the illustration in Fig. 11. This setup will accommodate one to five chicks. An adult chicken needs at least two square feet of space. The welded wire cage does nicely. They are expensive, so you might invest in the equipment shown in Fig. 18 before you spend a lot of money.

Temperature/Light/Humidity

The temperature will be regulated by your brood light. Position the light so that the floor temperature stays between 85 and 95 degrees Fahrenheit. Use no more than a 60-watt bulb. The warmth will be required until the chicks get older, possibly two weeks or more. They do well in room light and normal humidity.

Food and Water

Commercial feeds are best for growing chickens. Begin with something called chick start, which is a granular powder. As the chicks grow older, ten days to two weeks, use a hen scratch, which is a cracked corn. Chickens are omnivorous

and they will eat just about any food material. As adults, you can feed them chopped greens, dandelion greens, dandelion flowers, bread crumbs, and other light foods to establish a varied diet. Water should be supplied in a commercial chick watering dish which attaches to a glass jar. This type of water dish prevents the chicks from getting wet or even perhaps drowning. See Fig. 13.

Maintenance

You will find that chickens seem to produce more waste than the actual food they take in. It will be necessary to clean the cage at least once each day, sometimes twice, depending on the number of chicks you are keeping. Change and clean the water container daily.

Release and Disposal

Unfortunately, even the farmers don't need multiple roosters. Therefore it becomes quite a problem to find new homes for your pets. I would suggest you first contact a feed store in your area. Perhaps someone there raises chickens or in some way can take over the responsibility. You might also try your local high school and contact the person in charge of the vocational agriculture department.

Notes and Afterthoughts

Be careful not to put the food bowl in an area near your heat source. The chicks have a tendency to congregate and may actually trample or suffocate one another. Food should be kept available at all times as they will eat rather continuously and it causes them no harm. If your program advances to such a stage that the chicken is kept through its adulthood, you will need to check into a wire cage with a wire mesh floor and a metal tray, as this makes it easy to clean. You should be prepared to deal with a lot of noise because the hens cluck and the males crow.

Doves

Our two domesticated doves are the ring-necked and the
white dove. Doves make excellent cage animals for a
number of reasons. First of all they are not noisy. Although
they create a mess, it is not of the magnitude of other caged
birds. They are easily trained to do the one thing that I like
for birds to do and that is sit on your finger and not fly off.

Acquisition and Handling

Doves can be purchased at pet shops, feed stores, or you
can contact a local dove breeding organization. This
number can be obtained at your local zoo, feed store, or pet
shop as well. Doves don't peck or bite but are very nervous
animals. Move slowly toward them, then grasp gently, but
quickly, so as to pin their wings against their sides.

Cage and Habitat Materials

You should try to attain at least two square feet per dove. Your cage may be a fancy cockatiel or parrot cage, or you can use a welded wire rabbit cage turned on its long side and equipped with a perch or two. The perches should be about the diameter of a broomstick as doves have rather large feet and need the area for grasping. I have found that the hang-over-the-edge water and feeder work best for doves. Multi-layers of newspaper are a satisfactory substrate. If you are a handy person and are not into spending a lot of money for a cage, you might look into the materials illustrated in Fig. 18.

Temperature/Light/Humidity

Doves can be easily kept indoors at room temperature in available light and humidity. Avoid cold drafts, and if you keep your air conditioner below 65 degrees, you should cover the cage at night with a towel or sheet.

Food and Water

Doves do best on a varied diet. A partial list would be wild bird seed, finely chopped vegetables and fruits, earthworms, crickets, moths, and mealworms. They should be fed once each day. You will find that if you give them too much food, they will simply waste it by throwing it all over the place!

Maintenance

The cage should be dismantled and cleaned with a wire brush and a strong disinfectant such as Lysol or Clorox bleach at least once a week. The newspaper should be changed daily. A trick I use to control seed flinging is in the form of a paper skirt. Fold newspaper around the bottom of the cage and up the side about half way. Use hospital folds in the corners and secure with wooden clothespins. See the illustration in Fig. 14.

Release and Disposal

Ring-necked doves and white doves cannot make it in the wild. Contact the place where you originally got the bird and ask if they can help you find a home. You might also call your local elementary school as a possibility for a classroom pet, or call your local nature center.

Notes and Afterthoughts

As a precautionary measure, you might want to clip the bird's wings to avoid mishaps if he should try to escape. Your veterinarian or pet shop person can do this or show you how.

Ducks

Ah ducks! They come in all shapes and sizes. The most common are the white Pekin that you see in almost all city parks and lakes. The wild mallard is the second most common. They are yellow and black as babies. The white Pekin babies are yellow.

Acquisition and Handling

The only duck I would recommend keeping as a pet would be an orphan. The big white ducks in the park and the mallard ducks that frequent our park ponds sometimes find themselves in this situation. It is usually because of their close association with man. Mother and babies can become separated from being chased by people, dogs, cats, or sometimes big storms.

Ducklings are fragile creatures when first hatched and therefore handling be kept to a minimum. Ducklings are natural divers, not only in water, but also from a cradled hand. Hold them carefully.

Cage and Habitat Materials

A large cardboard box with many layers of paper on the bottom makes a good duck habitat. Cover half the top of the box with a sheet or towel to keep in heat and provide security. The box should be at least 24 inches deep.

Temperature/Light/Humidity

Ducklings need heat and this can be provided with a clamp-on reflector light fixture which can be purchased at the hardware store. Clamp the light on the box so that it is at least 18 inches from the floor of the box. The box should be large enough so that the ducklings can move away from the light should they become too hot. The temperature on the floor of the box should not exceed 90 degrees Fahrenheit.

Food and Water

All ducks are extremely messy eaters. Only experience will help you understand what they are capable of. Ducklings require high protein granulated food that you can purchase from any feed store. The food is generically known as game-bird starter or turkey start. This should be provided in a shallow bowl and decide what your duck will eat for one meal because they waste most of the food provided. Feed them once each day, preferably about the same time of the day. After six weeks or so, you may begin to add freshly chopped vegetables and cracked corn (sometimes called hen scratch) to their diet. Ducks eat just about anything, so you can supplement with bread crumbs, crackers, or about any food that is crumbly. A special treat would be fishing worms or small insects such as crickets.

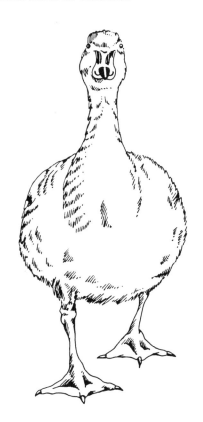

Water should be provided in a chick waterer that you can also purchase at the hardware store. See illustration in Fig. 13. They will empty the waterer as fast you fill it so it is necessary to check their water supply at least twice a day.

Maintenance

You can either clean and change the box once a day, or as soon as it becomes disgusting! The ducks think a mess is best! Try to remove the food dish as soon as they are through eating.

Release and Disposal

An adult duck, either white Pekin or mallard, will not be happy in your garage. If released in any local park pond, the duck will probably suffer greatly. Check with area property owners or farmers and try to find as isolated a location as you can.

Notes and Afterthoughts

Water and food containers should be placed as far as possible from each other. Although it is not necessary, the duck will go to great lengths to make a mush by mixing the food with the water and then sling it all over the room.

Pigeons

Pigeons are very common in any populated area and may be found roosting on roofs, telephone poles, or beneath bridges. They are disliked by most city officials because they are quite messy. They do make interesting pets and with enough room can be as intriguing as any other cage bird. Should you need to consult the reference books for more information, look for rock dove.

Acquisition and Handling

Pigeons may be obtained through the usual pet sources, but I have found if one waits long enough, a pigeon will pass through your life for one reason or another. Sometimes, when a pigeon is en route from one place to another, he will just tire out and he will land in a backyard or porch and refuse to leave. They also at various times in the spring will fly into a window. They are disoriented for a period of time and that is usually when a person will pick them up and take them in. A pigeon that has been in captivity for a period of time becomes quite docile, and handling is simply

a matter of pressing one's finger against the bird's chest and he will step onto your finger. Grabbing and removing a pigeon from somewhere is usually not necessary. If it becomes necessary, simply grasp the animal around both wings and body, then hold firmly but gently to avoid the animal harming himself by beating his wings against hard or sharp surfaces.

Cage and Habitat Materials

A good rule of thumb for a pigeon cage is at least two square feet per bird. A perch should be arranged near the direct center of the habitat. It should be about the diameter of a broomstick. Too small a perch is uncomfortable as is too large a perch. The cage should have a wire bottom that allows waste material to fall through to a substrate. The easiest substrate to maintain is newspaper in multiple layers. Cages are expensive and you may want to build your own. You'll need the material shown in Fig. 18.

Temperature/Light/Humidity

Pigeons can be maintained indoors with available light and normal room humidity. If you plan to be a serious pigeon person, you need to check into an outdoor coop, and there are a number of publications that will fit your needs and answer your questions.

Food and Water

Basic pigeon food can be purchased through commercial outlets and is a varied mixture of seeds and grains. You should also supplement this diet with chopped greens and canned mixed vegetables well drained. Clean water should always be available to your pet. Plastic water containers that hang from wires on the inside of the cage are very well suited for pigeons. They should be placed so that when the bird is sitting on its perch it will not accidentally defecate into the water.

Maintenance

The pigeon's cage should be dismantled and completely cleaned at least once a week. The substrate should be changed daily. It will be necessary to use a strong wire brush on the cage wire to clean it thoroughly. All uneaten food should be removed at the end of the day. It is very important that you feed them small amounts, as pigeons have a tendency to sling their food from side to side and will waste most of what you give them.

Release and Disposal

Releasing a pigeon into the wild can sometimes cause problems; therefore, it will be best to contact a local pigeon breeder for advice. They will sometimes take the bird, as they are always on the lookout for fresh stock. Your local nature center may also help find a new home.

Notes and Afterthoughts

Pigeons are by nature very messy birds. I have found that the mess can be kept to a minimum if you put a paper skirt beneath and up the side of the cage to about half way. This paper can be held in place using clothespins. It will keep all the thrown seed, water, and waste materials in a cleanable space. See the illustration in Fig. 14.

After you have had him in a cage for a month or so, he will become "homed" and will return to you from many miles away. Think about that.

Chapter 5
CRUSTACEANS

Predominately aquatic arthropods of the class Crustacea. Characteristically having a segmented body, a chitinous exoskeleton, and paired, jointed limbs.

Crayfish

Crayfish make an interesting aquarium display, and children really enjoy watching them eat. They mate in the fall. The sperm is stored in the female's body until spring when she lays several hundred eggs that have been fertilized by the stored sperm. The eggs attach to the little finger-like projections on the underside of her tail. They hatch in five to six weeks and the young will hang on for several more weeks until they are big enough to fend for themselves. They live for three to five years.

Acquisition/Handling

During the spring and summer, crayfish may be found in almost any longstanding body of water. They are easily netted or seined. Crayfish have very sharp pincers and it takes some practice to pick one up. Grasp the animal at the connection point between the carapace (top shell) and the abdomen on both sides of the back. Grasp firmly but gently as they will flip their tails violently in an effort to escape. Crayfish can also be purchased at some bait shops. It's a lot of fun to go "crawfishin'." All you need is a cane pole or a stick, some fishing line, and a strip of bacon. Find a low-lying area where you find some crawfish holes near the water. Tie the bacon on the line and let it slide down into the hole. Wait a few minutes and pull the line slowly and gently. Or, you can just toss the baited line into the water and again wait. Just before and during the molting process the crawfish will appear dead. Don't throw him out! After he has shed, it takes a few days for his exoskeleton to harden, so do not handle him during this time.

Cage and Habitat Materials

The 10-gallon aquarium is again the best container for your crawfish. You can go the elaborate route with plants, gravel, rocks, and stuff, or I would recommend that you use a bare aquarium without gravel or sand but including an air stone and a bottom filter. The water should be aged or bottled to avoid chemical contamination. Fill the aquarium to about four inches. Provide a rock that sticks out of the water because crayfish can drown if they can't get some air. See the setup in Fig. 22. They breathe with gills and they take in atmospheric oxygen.

Temperature/Light/Humidity

The water should be kept at room temperature and room light is sufficient.

Food and Water

The animals must be fed twice a week. They are carnivores and scavengers. The food list includes small chunks of liver, beef (no hamburger meat), fish, earthworms, minnows (dead), feeder goldfish, or guppies. These may be offered one piece at a time using tweezers. This will avoid clouding the water with uneaten food.

Maintenance

The water should be changed when it becomes cloudy. The air stone should be operating at full force at all times. Dismantle the entire habitat about once each month and clean with hot water and scrub brush, no soap.

Release and Disposal

Put them back into the creek during the warm months.

Notes and Afterthoughts

Crawfish can replace lost legs, pinchers, and eyes. If any of these break off, a series of sheddings will slowly grow them back!

Land-hermit Crabs or Tree Crabs

These crustaceans of the genus Coenobita are decapods (ten-legged). They use the front legs to climb, the second and third pairs to walk, and the fourth and fifth pairs to hang onto their adapted shell home and maneuver it while walking around. The exoskeleton is molted every twelve to fifteen months. During molting, the crab wants to hide and be left alone.

Born at sea, the baby comes ashore and looks for an abandoned shell for its home. The search for a better home never stops. They love to explore empty shells and change homes frequently.

Acquisition and Handling

They can be purchased at most pet shops. Choose a medium-sized animal. The small ones are delicate and the large ones may be old and ready to pass on. You will need one or two empty shells with circular openings as large or a little larger than the one the crab is now using. He will switch from one shell to another. Never shake him in his shell or try to remove him. He will allow himself to be torn apart rather than let go of his protective home. They can and do pinch, so avoid the claws.

Cage and Habitat Materials

A large goldfish bowl or aquarium with a screen top will serve nicely. Use sand or aquarium gravel about two inches deep for substrate. Add rock, driftwood, and plants (real or plastic). They love to climb, so provide a limb. Construct hiding places within the container.

Temperature/Lighting/Humidity

Keep the hermit crab away from direct sunlight and extremes of temperature. Room temperature should serve the animal well. Moisten the substrate every few days to keep the humidity constant.

Food and Water

Water should be provided in a shallow dish or jar lid. They eat almost anything. Commercial fish food is a good basic diet which may be supplemented with kale, apples, bananas, grapes, breakfast cereal, dry dog food, and peanut butter. Feed daily; their intake is less than you would expect. They may go for days without eating. Be sure to remove old food and keep the water fresh. They like moisture, so spray them lightly a few times each week.

Maintenance

Keep the cage area clean by removing uneaten food. Also clean the substrate every few weeks to remove the dirt.

Release and Disposal

Call your local elementary school and ask if they could use them. As a last resort, the pet shop where you got them will take them back.

Notes and Afterthoughts

No tree crabs have ever been bred in captivity. There are no obvious sexual differences, so you will just have to guess when you name them. They may live two to five years in captivity.

Pillbugs

The pillbug is a tiny land crustacean related to crabs and lobsters. They are also called rolly-pollies or sow bugs. These little animals are easily maintained in a small terrarium and require little care.

Acquisition and Handling

Pillbugs may be found in almost any moist area beneath rocks, boards, or other debris. They are nocturnal animals and can be found crawling about the leaf litter and on the foundation of your house during the warm months. They get their names because they roll up into a tight ball when disturbed. They are fragile creatures, so pick them up carefully. It may be best to place a container near the animal and simply brush him inside. They do not bite.

Cage and Habitat Materials

Any clear container that will hold two to three inches of moist soil will be sufficient. I use a one-gallon glass jar and punch only two or three holes in the lid as shown in Fig. 6. Add dead leaves and pieces of bark for cover.

Temperature/Light/Humidity

Pillbugs can be maintained at room temperature with available light. Humidity must remain high and will be indicated by condensation on the inside of the container. Mist the container with a plant atomizer about twice each week.

Food and Water

Pillbugs eat decaying plant material and can be fed green leafy vegetables, melon, apple, potato, shredded carrots and other greenery. They prefer decaying vegetation, so you can leave the food material in the container for a week at a time. Keep the substrate moist, but not wet, at all times.

Maintenance

To avoid fungal growth, it will be necessary to change the substrate about once a month or as needed. Remove all uneaten food at the end of each week.

Release and Disposal

This part is easy — put them back outside.

Notes and Afterthoughts

Under ideal conditions, these creatures will multiply rapidly. Pay close attention to various stages of growth and rest assured that all the different looking bugs in your habitat are the same kind of creature, just different ages.

Chapter 6
FISH

Cold-blooded aquatic vertebrates of the
superclass Pices. Characteristically having
fins, gills, and a streamlined body.

Fish

I am going to be quite frank about classroom and bedroom aquarium setups. You and I both know that interest wanes about the time the aquarium water turns green. So we are going to approach this matter as a temporary situation. A properly set up 10-gallon aquarium is a fascinating point of interest for young and old alike. We enjoy treating them as our television screen of nature. There are so many factors that affect the operation of this mini-habitat that one small change can affect the whole system. It is going to happen and be prepared for it!

Acquisition and Handling

Let's think inexpensive here and go through the garage sale route. You should be able to find your 10-gallon glass aquarium and a lot of the equipment for a small price after some other teacher or family lost interest. I will give you a list of basic materials:

- A 10-gallon aquarium or larger
- Underground filter with plastic corner tubes
- A few feet of plastic aquarium hose
- A two-way air valve (three-way gang valve)
- Small vibrator-type air pump
- Some sort of glass or plastic cover for the top of the aquarium
- An aquarium light (fluorescent or incandescent)
- An aquarium heater
- Three air stones, one for each corner of the filter and one for free air
- Three inches of bottom gravel (about 5 pounds)
- Plastic aquarium plants and rocks to please
- Water treatment to remove chloramines and chlorine
- Thermometer

Cage and Habitat Materials

This topic is only for consistency. We are going to discuss how to set it up! Fill your garage-sale aquarium full of water and let it sit for a day. It is a shame to go through all the elaborate setup and notice a puddle on the floor because your aquarium leaks. Insert the underground filter snugly on the bottom of the aquarium and then add the gravel. Using the water you let sit for a day, fill your aquarium to one inch from the top. Run one hose from the air pump to the main nozzle attachment of the gang valve. From the three valves in front of you, attach one hose from valve tip to corner tube of the bottom filter. This hose will attach to a stiff tube on the end of which there is an air stone. The middle gang valve should have a tube going to the free air stone. This air stone will be buried in the gravel, so please allow enough tubing for it. The last gang valve is likewise connected to the other corner of the underground filter. Attach the heater to the side of the aquarium. Add rocks and plants to your heart's content. Then fill the aquarium to the bottom lip of the top edge. Set the thermostat on the heater and mess with it till you obtain a water temperature of between 74 and 78 degrees Fahrenheit. When the proper temperature is reached, add the dechlorinating chemicals in the right amount and stir, not shake!

It would be safe to wait a day or two before you go to the pet shop to buy fish.

Temperature/Light/Humidity

As we have mentioned, the optimum temperature is between 74 and 78 degrees. Any abrupt changes in temperature can cause various health problems with your fish. The aquarium light should be turned off at night so as not to encourage algae growth or raise the temperature of the water. Also, some fish require a fixed photoperiod. The red sunlight will cause algae problems in your tank. Place the tank in a dark area of the room.

Food and Water

If you have questions at this point about how to give them water, maybe you should try gerbils instead! Food will depend upon your basic fish population, but generally a pinch of food daily is enough. When you think you have a pinch, give the fish about half of that! The worst enemy of aquarium maintenance is overfeeding.

Maintenance

Water evaporation will be a problem and you need to add water every day. A good idea is to keep a plastic gallon milk jug of treated water on hand for this purpose. The algae buildup on the inside of the glass can be eliminated by using some sort of straight edge on a stick to scrape off the algae. Your aquarium will last longer if you do a half-water change weekly. Simply dip or siphon about half the water from the aquarium and replace with aged and treated water. There are some considerations about ammonia, pH, and nitrate levels that are important if this turns into a lifetime situation! See your manuals or pet shop person for advice.

Release and Disposal

If all goes as is typical, in six to eight months you won't have any fish! As you can see by reading other chapters in this book, the aquarium makes an excellent small animal cage! If it becomes necessary to find homes for leftover fish, call your local school about a donation or neighbors that may have aquariums.

Notes and Afterthoughts

At this point we should do a fish list. The basic fish set would include fish that don't fight each other or eat their aquarium mates. You should not have more than twenty inches of fish in a 10-gallon tank. I will list the hardiest and most common and tell you a little about each:

Black mollies are live-bearers, one to two inches long.

Swordtails are live-bearers, two inches.

Tetra are egg-layers, one inch.

Cory cats are egg-layers, scavengers, two inches, you need two and they should not be included in the total inches of fish.

Pond snails eat algae or old food. Should they present a population problem just put in a live plant and they will gather on the leaves, then just heave the plant into the creek.

These fish and snails will live together just fine. The other common aquarium fish such as guppies, goldfish, angelfish, etc., each have some peculiarities so check with your pet shop fish person for more instructions.

Just being picky, when you screw down the plastic screws on both the gang valve and the heater, be careful not to tighten them too much; you will strip the screws. Don't leave the top uncovered because most fish have innate suicidal tendencies! The water will be cloudy when you first add it, so allow time for the filter to do its job. Try to attain equal release of air on both ends of the under-ground filter and the air stone. The smallest pump they make should run these three things together. Too large a pump and your fish will wear themselves out fighting the current, unless of course you have salmon!

The number of fish can be considered in inches. Twenty inches of fish for a 10-gallon aquarium with an under gravel filter. Twelve inches of fish with a plastic box type filter.

It is best to acclimate your fish to the tank water tempera-ture by floating the plastic bag containing the fish on top of the water for ten minutes. DO NOT FORGET THE FISH!

While we're talking tips, you might add one teaspoon of aquarium salt for each five gallons of water. It keeps the fish healthy.

Typical aquarium setup

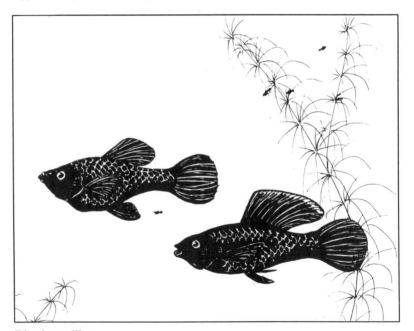

Black mollies

Neon tetra

Platy

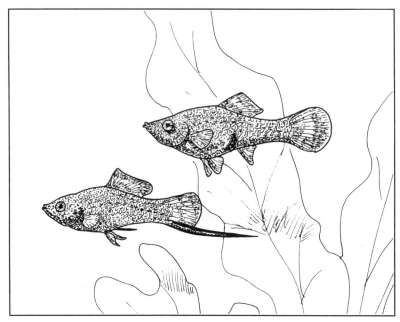

Sword tail

Cory cat

Chapter 7
LIZARDS

Reptiles of the suborder Sauria (or Lacertilia), characteristically having an elongated, scaly body, four legs, and a tapering tail.

Anoles (American Chameleon)

Remember when you visited the midway at the fair and you could buy a little green lizard on a string? Well, partly because of that you can now find them running along the outside walls of your house. Anoles are originally from Cuba and were shipped via the pet trade business to America.

Adult anoles grow to about six inches, including the tail. As the name chameleon indicates, they can change colors from dark green to dark brown and everything in between to match their surroundings, to hide from enemies, and also to absorb or reflect heat.

During the mating season the males will extend a bright orange or red flap of skin from beneath their throats and make push-up motions to attract females and to let other males know they have claimed their territory.

The female lays jelly-bean sized eggs in the soil and lets the sun incubate them. Young hatch in early summer and are miniature copies of the adults.

Since anoles are insect eaters, it is good to have them in your flower bed or garden.

Acquisition and Handling

Catching these lizards requires speed and agility and is, therefore, best left to the elementary school aged student. Take care in grabbing them because their tails break off easily. As with many lizards, the breakaway allows them to escape from predators. Anoles do bite when grabbed but the bite is much like a pinch as the teeth are not capable of breaking the skin.

A lizard noose is the easiest and safest way to capture small lizards. At the end of a fishing pole or long stick, attach a length of monofilament fishing line with a slip knot at the end as shown in Fig. 12. Approach the lizard from an angle and slip the noose over its head. Pull up quickly and the noose will tighten. This will not strangle or cut the animal because he is of such light weight.

Cage and Habitat Materials

A 10-gallon aquarium with a welded wire top makes an excellent habitat. For construction of that aquarium, see Fig. 9. The more habitat materials you put in the aquarium the more natural behavior will be exhibited. Small potted plants can be countersunk as well. Arrange small sticks to crisscross the inside and allow the anole to bask himself and be more easily accessible.

Temperature/Light/Humidity

Unfiltered sunlight is required for good health. You should let sunlight enter through the wire top for a period each day. The optimum habitat temperature is between 80 and 85 degrees F. A hot spot can be created by placing a light (25 to 50 watt) in a reflector globe on top of the aquarium as shown in Fig. 8. This allows the animal to move from hot

to cool as he needs. A 50-watt grow light on the cage top is sufficient for sunlight requirements if the animal is not kept too long.

Anoles prefer high humidity. This can be accomplished by using a large flat bowl for water. You should put a large rock in the bowl so the animal won't drown. You can also mist the habitat daily for extra moisture.

Food and Water

Water can be supplied by placing a shallow container of water in the bottom of the aquarium or by daily misting the inside walls and plants. Insects can be caught by using the insect trap illustrated in Fig. 3. Feed two or three insects per day. These should include crickets, mealworms, flies, moths, and roaches. If you keep them over winter, you can buy crickets and mealworms at the pet shop.

Maintenance

Keep the interior free of uneaten insects and wipe the sides clean with a damp paper towel. Do not use any type of household cleaner. If properly maintained, the anole can live from two to five years in captivity.

Release and Disposal

This is simple. Return him to the outdoors, preferably during late summer or early fall.

Notes and Afterthoughts

The male anole has a flap of skin beneath his throat called the dewlap. If these lizards are housed in a large terrarium with plants, sand, and lots of room, they may reproduce. The female will lay small jellybean-shaped eggs in the sand. The hatchlings look like miniature adults.

The hard skinned mealworms are not the best food for the anole because it might cause intestinal blockage over an extended period of time. Feed these only occasionally.

Caimans
(South American Alligators)

Caimans are native to Central and South America. There
are several species, some of which average six feet long.
They spend much of their time lying on the banks of
streams or floating underwater with only the tops of their
heads showing. They feed on all kinds of aquatic animals
and on any terrestrial animals caught at the water's edge. In
the summer twenty to thirty eggs are laid and incubated in
a nest by the heat of the decaying organic material. In some
species the female remains nearby to guard them through
the incubation period. The most common pet variety is the

spectacled caimen, so named because of a bony ridge between his eyes. He has the appearance of wearing glasses.

Acquisition and Handling

The baby spectacled caiman can be purchased in most pet shops when they are eight to twelve inches long. They are fast and ferocious. Picking one up, if you must, requires one quick grab behind the jaws in front of the shoulders. If you miss, and it gets you, it will bite, hold on, and twist its body violently. It has sharp teeth and remarkably strong jaws.

Cage and Habitat Materials

Fill a 10-gallon aquarium to about two inches over the top of the animal's back with tap water. Place a large flat rock at one end of the tank so the animal can crawl on it and be completely out of the water. Cover the tank with a welded wire screen as shown in Fig. 23. They are escape artists.

Temperature/Light/Humidity

Place a reflector-type lamp fixture on the wire over the end of the tank where the rock is located. Use a 50-watt plant grow reflector bulb as shown in Fig. 8. Before you put the caiman in the tank, use an outdoor thermometer to measure the temperature on the top of the rock. It should read 85 to 90 degrees Fahrenheit.

Food and Water

Caimans enjoy a wide variety of foods. Goldfish or minnows can be released live in the water. Feed at least two food items daily. Use tweezers or tongs to offer pink mice or sliced mouse, bits of lean meat, crickets, mealworms, or chicken livers. Do not leave uneaten food in the tank as it will foul the water.

Maintenance

Change the water at least twice each week or more often as needed. Wash the rock with a scrub brush. Don't use soap on the inside of the tank. Use hot water and elbow grease only.

Release and Disposal

There will be some difficulty here. Caimans are not native and should not be released in local waterways. Call a nature center in your area or contact your nearest herpetological society for advice in disposal. You can locate that organization through the local zoo.

Notes and Afterthoughts

Caimans are fascinating as babies, but as they get older and bigger there will be problems. Although the size of the habitat can stunt or slow their growth, in five years you will have a dangerous animal on your hands. Try to borrow one for a while.

I do not recommend these animals for classroom or bedroom pets!

Fence Lizards

These are small gray or brown lizards with strong tree-climbing tendencies. Males and females are easily distinguished by the males' brilliant blue underside. The scales are arranged to look much like shingles on a roof. There are a variety of species ranging in size from four inches to almost a foot. They make good temporary captives and can be released locally.

Acquisition and Handling

You may use a lizard noose as shown in Fig. 12 or any third-grader can catch one! They do wiggle a lot and the trick is to catch one with his tail intact. The breaking off of the tail is one of the primary defense mechanisms of these lizards. Although it will regenerate and grow back, it takes a long time and they look a little silly in the meantime. These lizards may be found blending in with the vertical side of trees and fence posts. Their bite is not much more than a pinch but it is enough to cause a flying lizard!

Cage and Habitat Materials

The 10-gallon aquarium setup with a wire top is best for this lizard. Look at wire tops in Fig. 21. Habitat materials should consist of as many branches as you can get in the cage. The substrate may be clean sand or topsoil. A hiding place can be provided by firmly stacking flat rocks in a corner.

Temperature/Light/Humidity

As a temporary captive, this lizard will do well at room temperature with available light and humidity supplied by a large water dish. Keep in mind that their activities are directed by the temperature: the warmer, the more active, the cooler, the more dormant. These lizards do hibernate during the winter and will become less active during the cold months. You probably should avoid keeping them through the winter. Heat may be provided using any of the setups shown in Fig. 7, Fig. 8, or Fig. 11. The optimum temperature is between 85 and 90 degrees Fahrenheit.

Food and Water

I feed my fence lizards live crickets, roaches, and corn grubs. Some of the larger species eat baby mice. See the insect trap shown in Fig. 3. These food items should be offered daily and you should remove uneaten food at the end of the day. Water should be provided in a shallow dish and kept clean and filled at all times. They also enjoy licking droplets of water off of their habitat materials. This may be done with a plant atomizer about once each day.

Maintenance

Waste materials can be removed from the substrate with a spoon or tweezers. Do not allow any food item to remain in the cage for more than a few hours. The entire habitat should be dismantled and cleaned when it begins to look scroungy. Use a mild dishwashing soap and rinse thoroughly.

Release and Disposal

Try to release the animal in the area where you found it. Release during the warm months to allow time for seeking a hibernating spot.

Notes and Afterthoughts

To avoid drowning the crickets fed to the lizards and having them foul the drinking water, put a stone in the center of the water dish so the crickets can haul out.

Geckos

Every time I get a gecko I name him "Jose"! Geckos are delicate little four- to five-inch long lizards. They have big beautiful eyes and when they wink it almost makes you blush. Don't count on it because not all of them have eyelids. Their scales are bumpy and have a velvet-like surface. Some have small pads on their feet that aid in their climbing almost anything. Colors vary. They are nocturnal animals and may be found on walls near lights that attract insects on which they feed. There are several different species in the southern United States but care and maintenance is about the same for all.

Acquisition and Handling

As I mentioned, you will find these animals at night on an outdoor wall near a light. Their tails break easily, so the less you handle them the better for the lizard. I would recommend using the lizard noose as shown in Fig. 12 to catch this animal. Trying to trap them under your hand might result in a squashed lizard or a wiggling tail and no lizard!

Cage and Habitat Material

The 10-gallon aquarium with the wire screen top will do nicely for a habitat. See the illustration in Fig. 9. Use gravel, sand, or soil for a substrate to a depth of about two inches. Geckos like vertical surfaces and will spend a lot of time simply stuck to the glass. You might also arrange flat rocks so they are vertical but will not fall.

Temperature/Light/Humidity

Geckos require both heat and light for health. Arrange your heat source so that one end of the habitat is between 78 and 85 degrees Fahrenheit and the other end is cooler. Heat may be supplied by using the methods shown in Fig. 8 or Fig. 11. Sunlight or artificial light will be needed. Allow indirect sunlight to shine through the top of the cage. You can also put a black light tube across the top of the habitat. A temporary substitute may be a 50-watt grow light or plant light in your heat source. The black light should only be left on for eight hours during the day so he won't OD on UV!

You should mist the habitat with a plant sprayer at least once each day.

Food and Water

Geckos eat live insects. You can catch plenty of live food by using the trap shown in Fig. 3. Offer two or three food items each day and more if he eats them all. You may purchase crickets at the bait store. Avoid feeding mealworms because they will have trouble digesting the hard shell. This would be a good time to consider raising roaches.

Supply water in a shallow container such as a jar lid. They prefer to lap water off the sides of the rocks or glass.

Maintenance

Remove uneaten food at the end of the day. Dismantle the habitat about every two weeks. Wash with mild detergent and rinse thoroughly. Wash the rocks with hot water and a brush. Don't use soap on the rocks. Clean and fill the water dish daily.

Release and Disposal

Try to release the animal where you found him. They hibernate, so release them during the warm season. If he was shipped in from elsewhere, you might call the local zoo and ask about herpetological societies in your area. There you can find a home for your captive.

Notes and Afterthoughts

It is best to keep one gecko per habitat just to be on the safe side.

Glass Lizards

"If you drop them, they will break into a hundred pieces! After dark they sneak back and grow together again." So goes the old story about this lizard with no legs. Make no mistake about it, they are lizards. Watch their eyes. They can blink with eyelids. Snakes don't have eyelids. The glass lizard also has ear holes whereas snakes do not. The scales all around the glass lizard are the same size. Snakes have a different sized belly scales and back scales. They won't break into many pieces, but they will break off their tails in an effort to escape. This is common in most of our North American lizards. They are fun to watch and even more interesting to explain.

Acquisition and Handling

These animals may be collected in grassland areas or dry woodlands. Look under leaf piles, logs, boards, and other debris. It is best to use the hand-trap method. Simply slap a flat hand over the animal and then pick him up while supporting as much of his body as possible. They are not biters but will squirm frantically. They are most easily transported in a cloth bag.

Cage and Habitat Materials

Use the 10-gallon aquarium and light setup as shown in Fig. 8. Fill the aquarium with two to three inches of sand or topsoil. Add dry leaves and pieces of bark to provide a hiding place.

Temperature/Light/Humidity

Use a 60-watt light bulb and raise the temperature of one end of the aquarium to 85 degrees Fahrenheit. Spray the habitat with a plant atomizer about once a week. If you plan to keep this animal for extended periods, it will require a black light or some form of indirect, unfiltered sunlight. The black light tube will fit the standard aquarium light fixture and can be placed on top of the habitat. It should be turned on for only four to six hours each day. You don't want your lizard to OD on UV!

Food and Water

Glass lizards eat a variety of small creatures which include worms, insects, and even small mice. Feed your lizard crickets, earthworms, and the insects you catch in your insect trap shown in Fig. 3. Feed two or three food items daily. Remove the uneaten food at the end of the day. Provide a shallow water dish and keep it clean and full at all times.

Maintenance

Waste material can be spooned from the soil as often as it occurs. The habitat should be dismantled and cleaned with a mild detergent about every two weeks. Don't be concerned if the lizard refuses to eat for a few days after you clean the cage. He has to get used to the new arrangement.

Release and Disposal

Release the lizard where you found him or somewhere similar in habitat and climate. Glass lizards hibernate, so release them during the summer months.

Notes and Afterthoughts

Just to be safe, let this animal have the habitat all to himself. He likes it that way.

Iguanas

The common green iguanas are found throughout Mexico and into South America. These very large green lizards can grow to six feet which is mostly tail. They are imported for the pet trade and suffer greatly at the hands of well-meaning pet buyers. They are very agile tree climbers, and as most owners would agree, they enjoy heights! They are more delicate and require more specialized care than the animal sellers will admit.

Acquisition and Handling

The green iguana is sold in most pet shops and will usually be a juvenile not more than six to eight inches long. Most reputable pet shops will have healthy animals, but there is a problem. As youngsters, they require extreme care right down to and including hand-feeding. Choose an animal that is bright-eyed, not showing any ribs, no discharge around the mouth or nose, uniform scales and, most importantly, has use of all four limbs! An iguana with unusually fat thighs is not necessarily healthy — this may be a swollen condition from improper calcium intake. Iguanas are tree-dwelling animals, and when allowed to run they go for heights, which usually means the top of your head or a curtain rod. They are quite fidgety and must be held firmly but gently. You will suffer the most damage from their claws and they hardly ever bite. When your iguana reaches three to four feet in length you will have learned to approach slowly, quietly and to allow the iguana to seek his own hold. My largest lizards seem to enjoy hanging from the front of my shirt and riding around.

Cage and Habitat Materials

Iguanas need a lot of room the larger the cage, the happier and the healthier the iguana. You may start out in a 10-gallon aquarium with a lizard eight to twelve inches long and then increase as he grows! For a six-foot adult, I have a five by five by eight foot wire enclosure with trees and logs for climbing. This size can be easily constructed with the equipment shown in Fig. 18. Sunlight is necessary and a basking area is a requirement. A horizontal log at a slight angle will allow the animal to stretch out to enjoy the heat and light.

I use multi-layers of newspaper on the cage floor. This seems to be the safest because they have a tendency to eat anything else.

Temperature/Light/Humidity

I have found that temperatures between 88 and 95 degrees Fahrenheit at all times keep your creature healthy and happy. They also require high humidity, and this can be difficult in a wire cage. I keep a plant atomizer handy and spray as frequently as time allows. A large shallow water pan should be provided to allow for bathing and soaking. Unfiltered sunlight is an absolute requirement. Your entire habitat should be placed half in the sun and half in the shade for as many hours of the day as is practical. During the cold months, artificial light is necessary. This may be provided in the form of a black light tube on top of the habitat. The black light should be on a timer set for twelve hours on and twelve off. Heat should be supplied by use of an infrared lamp close enough to the cage to provide heat but not so close as to blister the animal. I do not recommend a "hot rock" because the iguana has a weird nervous system and will fry himself before he will move off a hot spot. The pet store has any number of different lights that will satisfy your iguana's ultraviolet requirements.

Food and Water

Iguanas are almost entirely herbivorous and will eat all manner of fruit and vegetables. A large portion of their diet should be green leafy material. The grocery list is as follows: mustard greens, turnip greens, collard greens, carrot tops, and parsley. You may include minimal amounts of kale and romaine lettuce. The fruit and vegetable list consists of: grapes, kiwi, strawberries, cantaloupe, banana, blueberries, pineapple, and fruit cocktail. Drained canned mixed vegetables can be given as well as sliced yellow squash, zucchini, okra, carrots, and yams.

Mix as many of these ingredients in one salad as possible because iguanas can be finicky eaters. If you find that your critter tends to eat only his favorite item, try to lessen the amount of that item to stimulate his consumption of the healthy stuff. There are a number of vitamin supplements on the market specifically for iguanas. If, for some reason, your iguana does not respond to the recommended light, humidity, cage, and diet that you have provided, by all means use a supplement.

Water should be supplied in a large shallow pan at all times.

Maintenance

Change paper in the habitat at least twice a week; remove all uneaten food at the end of the day. Dismantle the habitat at least once each month and clean all parts and materials with a mild dishwashing soap. Rinse thoroughly. The water pan should be cleaned and refilled daily.

Release and Disposal

Unless you live in Mexico or South America don't release him! Call your local zoo, and right after they say no, ask if one of the keepers would like to have an iguana. I hesitate to recommend checking with the pet shops as they will take him in and sell him again to who knows whom! You might contact your local college biology department, but before you release your iguana to them, be sure they don't have dissection in mind!

Notes and Afterthoughts

When your iguana appears very tame and part of the family, you will be tempted to allow him to roam freely. Keep in mind these lizards will eat anything small enough to get in their mouths. Many iguanas have suffered injury and illness because of little things they pick up under the refrigerator. There has been some recent concern with a bacterium called salmonella that is present naturally on the skin of most reptiles. Try to remember to simply wash your hands after handling any animal.

Prairie Skinks

These quick little snake-like lizards can be seen scampering across the leaf tops in a real big hurry. They grow to eight inches long and have stripes — the center body stripe being the widest. The males are a deep reddish-orange on the sides of their heads particularly during breeding season. They are seldom seen in the open. They occur in areas of soft sand or soil or in the forests under the dead leaf litter.

Acquisition and Handling

The primary defense mechanism of the skink is to break off its tail and then take off while you watch the wiggle! I use the quick-grab technique, whereby you get the lizard, the leaves, the dirt, the twigs and occasionally something called stinging nettle! Separate those items carefully and hopefully you will come up with a skink.

Cage and Habitat Materials

The plastic shoe box or sweater box makes the ideal mini-habitat as shown in Fig. 5. The substrate should be sand or soil covered with dead leaves.

Temperature/Light/Humidity

Situate your habitat in any area with indirect sunlight. Humidity may be maintained by misting the leaves about every other day. They do well at temperatures between 75 and 80 degrees Fahrenheit.

Food and Water

Provide water in a shallow dish. Food items should include earthworms, pillbugs, small slugs, ground-dwelling insects, small crickets, and other insects you can catch in your back porch insect trap shown in Fig. 3. Feed one or two food items each day.

Maintenance

Remove dead or uneaten insects at the end of each day. Dismantle and thoroughly clean the habitat at least once every two weeks. Wash with a mild dishwashing soap and rinse thoroughly.

Release and Disposal

Release the animal at or near the site of capture. Be sure and release during the warmer months as they do hibernate and need time to find their spot.

Notes and Afterthoughts

Keep handling to a minimum because broken tails are unsightly and it makes observers melancholic!

Savannah Monitors

The African savannah monitor is one of the smaller of the monitor family and grows to about three feet long. The youngsters which appear in pet shops have a beautiful pattern and a nippy disposition. As they get older they get less nippy and uglier gray. They are close relatives of the Kommodo dragon and the kids love to hear you say that. I do not encourage you to purchase reptiles at pet shops, but if you do, use the following information to save it from almost certain death.

Acquisition and Handling

If you save one of these lizards from someone who does not know how to care for him, it will appear to be the most laid-back, friendliest lizard you have ever met. That may be indicative of starvation, dehydration, and other things. If he is lively and healthy, you'd best grasp him behind the head and in front of the front feet with one hand, and at the same time, grab the tail at the rear of the back legs. They have long claws, so watch the feet! Don't grab them solely by the tail because although it doesn't break off as easily as with other lizards, it is rather weak towards the tip.

Cage and Habitat Materials

Any monitor under ten inches may be housed nicely in a 10-gallon aquarium setup as shown in Fig. 9. I find it best to use multi-layers of cut newspaper for a substrate. You may choose soil or gravel to a depth of at least four inches.

Temperature/Light/Humidity

Monitors do best in a temperature range from 80 to 88 degrees Fahrenheit. This may be accomplished using any of the heating techniques shown in Fig. 7, Fig. 8, or Fig. 11. If you contemplate a long-term captive, they do require some ultraviolet light. This may be supplied with a black light tube on top of the habitat or by placing the habitat in indirect sunlight for a few hours each day. To avoid overdosing with the UV, the light should be left on only four to six hours for every twenty-four hours. Humidity may be supplemented by misting the animal about every third day.

Food and Water

Monitors are carnivorous so I will give you a partial list of food items. Sliced raw chicken, chopped chicken necks, dead (frozen and thawed) mice, raw liver, and minimum amounts of lean red beef will round out his diet and his body very nicely. The food may be offered with forceps in bite-sized chunks; do not offer the lizard live food! Water should be supplied in a dish large enough for him to submerge his entire body.

Maintenance

The entire habitat should be dismantled and cleaned with a mild dishwashing soap at least once each week. The water dish should be cleaned and refilled daily.

Release and Disposal

These are African animals that cannot live in a North American climate. Do not release them in the woods. Here is a brief list of potential caretakers: local herpetological society members, university teachers of biology, grade school teachers, local nature center, and last a pet shop.

Notes and Afterthoughts

Monitors will lay across a hot rock even if it has gone haywire and becomes a grill. If you use a hot rock, check it daily to see that it does not overheat. Monitors are rather aggressive at feeding time and they are terrible shots, so watch your fingers.

Six-lined Race Runners

They belong to a large family of lizards called whiptails. There are nine other species that occur in our area; all are diurnal and may be recognized by the long tails and active nervous prowling. These creatures grow from six to ten inches long and have stripes of yellow, white, pale gray, or pale blue. They are very active lizards and prefer open well-drained areas covered with sand or loose soil. The race runners are well-named because they can outrun any nine-year-old on foot!

Acquisition and Handling

These are best collected with a lizard noose as shown in Fig. 12. Practice slow, deliberate movements until you are close enough. They should be handled with great care as the tails break off easily, leaving you with a wiggling tail and no lizard. Early morning and late evenings you'll find them under rocks, boards, or other flat debris.

Cage and Habitat Materials

The 10-gallon aquarium and light setup as shown in Fig. 9 will do nicely. A general rule is one lizard per habitat. The substrate should be dry sand or loose topsoil. They are secretive animals and should be provided with a place to hide; for example, a flat rock leaning against a round rock or something similar. Imagination will take care of it and be your guide! If you really like a lot of rocks, be careful not to stack them loosely as one fall might kill all!

Temperature/Light/Humidity

Race runners like it hot! The substrate temperature should be around 90 degrees Fahrenheit. Their food items supply most of the water they need and they really prefer very dry conditions. Short-term captives require only heat, but for periods of over a month, a black light should be placed on top of the aquarium. If possible they need a few hours of indirect unfiltered sunlight each day.

Food and Water

Race runners are insectivores and do nicely on crickets, grubs, and back porch light insects that you can catch with the trap illustrated in Fig. 3. Water may be offered in a jar lid which must be changed daily as the lizards will fill it with sand or dirt. Remove all uneaten food at the end of the day, and they should be offered food daily.

Maintenance

Waste material can be spooned from the substrate on a daily basis. The substrate should be changed every two weeks as needed. A change in habitat material positions may upset the lizard and he may refuse to eat for a short period of time. Take heart — he'll get over it!

Release and Disposal

Release these lizards where you found them or at least into similar habitats and climates. Release during the warm months as they do hibernate and will need time to find their spot.

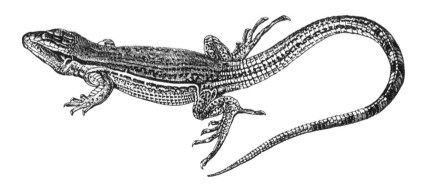

Notes and Afterthoughts

More than one lizard in close quarters can elicit strange behaviors such as cannibalism and such intimidation that neither animal will eat or drink. You should also avoid putting the aquariums side by side, because sometimes just the sight of another lizard will provoke territorial reactions.

Chapter 8
MAMMALS

A class of vertebrate animals of more than 15,000 species. Distinguished by self-regulating body temperature, hair, and, in the females, milk-producing mammae.

Chinchillas

A chinchilla looks like a cross between a rabbit and a dormouse and has fur that is unimaginably soft. Its natural habitat is high in the Andes mountains of South America. Chinchillas are rodents and belong to the same group as rats, mice, and guinea pigs.

Acquisition and Handling

Chinchillas can be purchased at pet shops and are usually pretty expensive. They are rather hyperactive and hard to catch. I usually grab them by the tail and then lay their body across my hand. Don't squeeze!

Cage and Habitat Materials

I've had chinchillas over the years and each has been healthy and happy in a two-by-two-foot square welded wire cage. The cage is expensive, so you may want to invest in the equipment shown in Fig. 18 and build your own. You can make a space beneath for a sliding pan, and that makes cleaning easier. I purchased a metal rabbit feeder bin that goes through the wire. This avoids the spills and mess from a bowl.

Temperature/Light/Humidity

Chinchillas are cold-weather animals. Their fur is an excellent insulator. They must be kept in an air-conditioned space. They prefer between 65 and 72 degrees Fahrenheit. Room light and humidity will suffice.

Food and Water

Chinchillas eat rabbit pellets which you can supplement with fresh veggies such as carrot, sweet potato, and kale. Keep the pellets available at all times. Feed the supplements only once daily and in small amounts. A rabbit-type water bottle can be used.

Maintenance

Chinchillas require "dust" baths about three times a week. The dust may be purchased at the pet store. Put about one inch in a bowl large enough that the chinchilla can climb into and turn freely in. I take the bowl out after a couple of hours, because he will sling the dust all over the place!

Release and Disposal

Don't release them into the wild! You can ask a teacher to take him on as a classroom pet with an adoption option. The pet shop will gladly take him for resale. I have found homes through newspaper ads.

Notes and Afterthoughts

There are volumes written about chinchillas because they are valued for their pelts. You don't really want to breed them for sale, you just think you do.

Ferrets

The ferret is a member of the weasel family. It is a long, strongly built, sleek animal. It is physically adapted to finding food in burrows. In nature, they eat ground-dwelling rodents, primarily prairie dogs, and the European varieties eat rabbits. Used as a verb, to "ferret" out describes the way this animal hunts. European hunters have trained these animals to flush rabbits from their burrows. Ferrets make mediocre pets because of their intense curiosity and tendencies to rip and tear.

Acquisition and Handling

Ferrets may be purchased at pet shops. A possible better source would be to contact any one of the number of ferret associations which you may find in your phone book. Ferrets are carnivorous creatures and, therefore, have a formidable set of teeth. Bites can range from the playful nip to a tenacious death grip. For example, I once had a large male ferret attach itself between my thumb and forefinger. I

used my always successful thumb-to-the-nose technique which had no effect. I eventually had to fill the sink with water and immerse ferret, fist, and all until he finally let go. Ferrets should be allowed to leave their cages before being picked up. They are most likely to nip and bite while still in the cage. Grasp the animal from above, around the shoulders and neck. Support the rest of his body with your other hand. I have found that ferrets frequently lick a spot of skin before biting it.

Cage and Habitat Materials

If your ferret gets exercise on a daily basis outside the cage, the space requirements are minimal. A two-by-two-foot square welded wire cage, preferably with a raised wire bottom and waste tray, should be sufficient. A ferret will use a kitty litter box if it is placed in the corner he chooses as a bathroom. A hidebox built of light wood with an appropriate sized hole is a welcome addition. All ferrets love a towel to wrap themselves in. This towel should be made of terry cloth and considered disposable once they stay in it for a week. You may easily construct your own wire cage by using the materials illustrated in Fig. 18.

Temperature/Light/Humidity

Ferrets do nicely in the same environment that you enjoy.

Food and Water

A good basic diet that seems to be enjoyed by all ferrets is Meow Mix by Ralston Purina. You might also try various wet and dry cat/dog foods to find one he really likes. Water should be provided with an outside hanging rabbit-type of water bottle. A water bowl would simply be overturned and cause a big mess. Feed daily as you would your dog or cat. Remove uneaten food after a few hours.

Maintenance

The wire cage should be emptied and thoroughly brushed clean using a strong disinfectant at least once a week. The litter and pan should be changed daily.

Your ferret can be bathed occasionally and this will help control the odor. You can use a mild pet shampoo.

Release and Disposal

Unfortunately, when you buy a ferret, nobody wants it but you. In this order, I would recommend you call your local nature center, a few pet shops, or that ferret organization that recommended him in the first place. Do not release this animal in the woods as he is semi-domesticated and cannot fend for himself.

Notes and Afterthoughts

Some city ordinances prohibit keeping ferrets as pets. Check there first. Ferrets are very susceptible to distemper and therefore need vaccination. Since they can be biters you should have your ferret vaccinated for rabies.

Gerbils

Gerbils are mouse-like creatures about six inches long, tail included. They are rodents and have gnawing front teeth. They come in all colors: white, black, black and white, and black and brown. Most common is light brown. Gerbils are easy to care for and don't smell as bad as some of the other choices of pets for the bedroom or classroom. Sift through your local pet shop's population and look for two young gerbils. I say two because they seem to be happier with a playmate. If you don't want to start your own pet shop I suggest you get two brothers or sisters. Look for bright eyes, full fur, long tail, dry nose, and good muscle tone.

Acquisition and Handling

Gerbils are the most common pet shop acquisition. The easiest, safest way to pick up a gerbil is to grasp it quickly by the tail and lay its body across your open hand. Squeezing or grabbing the animal by the body may cause him to bite.

Cage and Habitat Materials

The 10-gallon aquarium is the best container. A welded wire top or plastic and screen wire top will do to keep this animal contained. See the illustration in Fig. 21. A water bottle can be wired to hang over the inside edge of the aquarium. Litter may be anything from commercially produced cedar chips to strips of newspaper. The key to a happy gerbil seems to be the depth of litter. They do best in three to four inches of material in the aquarium.

Avoid the use of exercise wheels because they might cause injury to the animal. Hiding places and toys should be supplied in the form of toilet paper rolls and empty shoe boxes with holes cut through the sides. A typical gerbil habitat is shown in Fig. 16.

Temperature/Light/Humidity

Room temperature is good and you should avoid extremes of heat and cold. Ordinary light and average humidity will suffice. Do not allow the animal to become damp if the substrate gets wet from a leaky water bottle.

Food and Water

Your local grocery store will have a variety of commercially produced gerbil food. These are nutritionally sufficient, and your pet will thrive with only this kind of food. For happiness and health, you may supplement with bits of vegetable and fruit such as carrots, apples, potatoes, but *not* lettuce, which is nutritionally vacant and causes diarrhea. Feed daily and in small amounts and remove uneaten food at the end of the day.

Water should be supplied with a hanging water bottle on the inside of the aquarium. Check these frequently because they have a tendency to either stop up or leak. Gerbils are desert animals and do not require a lot of water.

Maintenance

Gerbils are naturally clean animals. They don't urinate very much and when they do it is usually in one particular corner of the habitat. It is a simple matter to use a large spoon and dip out the waste material. Take care not to leave uneaten food in the habitat, particularly if it was fresh vegetables or fruits. The entire habitat should be taken apart and cleaned with a mild dishwashing liquid at least once each month and more often if needed.

Release and Disposal

If and when the gerbil requires a change in situation, check with the following people in this order: friends, neighbors, teachers, pet shop owners, and then just keep it yourself! They live two to four years.

Notes and Afterthoughts

Never under any circumstances release this animal into the woods! They cannot survive in the wild and this certainly would mean cruel and unusual punishment.

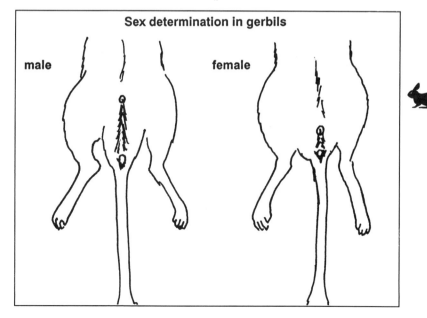

Sex determination in gerbils
male   female

Guinea Pigs

Thought to be descended from a wild animal the Incas kept nearly 500 years ago, these rodents are still raised as a food source in South America. They are the perfect first pet for young children because of their docile nature and ease in handling. They vary in color and coats, making each one unique. They may get the name pig from the oinking sound they make when they are hungry, exited, or want attention.

Acquisition and Handling

If purchased from a pet shop, the guinea pig should be from six to eight weeks old. Look for alert, fully furred, bright-eyed animals. Feel around on their skin for lumps and knots. Also, check the tail area to make sure the fur is dry. Either sex makes a good pet, and two of them of the same sex will be compatible if put together when young. To pick up, place one hand on the top at the shoulders and place the other hand underneath the animal. They will bite if squeezed or pinched.

Habitat

There are two types of cages suitable for long-term care. The better one is a plastic pan base with a coated wire, removeable cage top. It may be purchased at a pet shop. The second type is an aquarium, 10-gallon or larger, with a welded wire top as shown in Fig. 16. Use cedar chips or pine shavings for the substrate. The disadvantage to this cage is that the entire contents must be changed more often. A water bottle purchased at a pet shop can be mounted on the outside of the wire cage and on the inside rim of the aquarium.

Being rodents, they must gnaw on things to keep their teeth from growing too long. Give them a chunk of good hard wood such as pecan or maple.

Temperature/Light/Humidity

Room temperature is good, avoiding too much heat. Warmer climates do not permit them to be kept outdoors. Ordinary light and average humidity will suffice. Do not allow the animal to become damp. The substrate can become wet from a leaky water bottle. Keep the habitat out of drafts as this will cause serious health problems.

Food and Water

Guinea pig pellets may be purchased at the pet shop or in some of the larger grocery stores. This special diet includes vitamin C which is essential to health. An occasional supplement to the pellets can be fresh vegetables or good quality hay or alfalfa. Keep food available at all times but remove uneaten food at the end of the day. Clean the water bottle regularly and keep filled.

Maintenance

Guinea pigs will keep themselves clean if you keep their surroundings clean. There are sometimes problems with nails and teeth. After the animal is one year old the nails may need to be cut. Using nail clippers, cut only the tips, being sure that they are a pale color and not red or brown. Cutting too much will cause a lot of bleeding. Check teeth regularly to be sure they are not growing too long and preventing the animal from eating. If there is a problem, the veterinarian can do the clipping.

If using an aquarium, the cage litter should be completely changed every other day to avoid odors.

Release and Disposal

If the time comes when you must give the pet away and you haven't been successful asking friends, try calling your child's teacher or any school and ask to donate the animal as a classroom pet. Suggest that the animal needs a good home and is up for adoption.

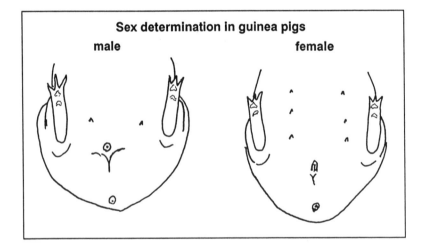

Sex determination in guinea pigs

male   female

Hamsters

These cute little bear-like mammals make interesting and exciting classroom or bedroom pets. You will hear them called by many names. There are golden, teddy bear, Chinese dwarf, and Russian dwarf. The differences are size, color, and hair length. Hamsters are rodents that have cheek pouches. They will stuff them with food and take it to a storage area where they dump it.

Acquisition and Handling

The pet store will have lots of hamsters. Look for bright eyes, clean nose, dry tail, all their hair, and some youth. Check their teeth to make sure they are not too long. You must spend some time getting a new hamster accustomed to your hand before you attempt a pick-up. Touch and stroke a lot. Pick them up with thumb on one side and fingers on the other about mid-body. Don't try to pick them up as they are just waking up. They do not like it!

Cage and Habitat Materials

The 10-gallon aquarium as shown in Fig. 16 will make the perfect hamster habitat. Fill to three inches with cedar or pine shavings. These can be purchased at the grocery store. They enjoy exploration, so provide paper rolls or a shoe box with big holes. They are escape artists, so the top must be secure. The plastic and screen tops will screw down (see Fig. 21) but the screws will strip, so check them occasionally. Buy a small bottle waterer that hangs in a bracket on the inside of the aquarium.

Temperature/Light/Humidity

They do well at standard room light, temperature, and humidity. Avoid placing the cage in drafty places or in front of an air-conditioning vent.

Food and Water

Keep the water bottle clean and full at all times. They enjoy a variety of foods and should be fed a small amount every day. Their food list includes: seeds, nuts, rat blocks, commercial gerbil/hamster food, and some fresh veggies such as carrot, apple, potato, and kale.

Maintenance

The entire habitat will need to be dismantled about once each month and scrubbed. Use a mild dishwashing soap and rinse well. They use one corner for a bathroom, so you should dip out the waste daily. They use another corner for food storage, and that should be removed at the end of the week so you don't grow things other than hamsters.

Release and Disposal

You cannot let them go in the woods, so start asking around. Call a school teacher for a possible donation with an adoption option. A newspaper ad will sometimes work. As a last resort take them to a pet shop.

Notes and Afterthoughts

To avoid fights and more hamsters than you can handle, just keep one hamster per habitat.

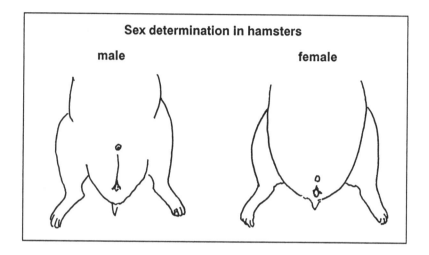

Sex determination in hamsters

male   female

Hedgehogs

The African pygmy hedgehog came onto the pet scene in the mid-1980s. These six-inch-long insectivores (eats mostly insects and worms) can be good pets. Keep in mind that you really must love them to put up with their instinctual behavior. I suggest you check out and read some of the comprehensive material about them before you make the commitment. It is difficult to find a new home for this quirky little mammal.

Acquisition and Handling

CAUTION: Check that you will not be breaking any local laws or regulations.

Check out the pet shop population very carefully before you purchase. Look closely at the usual stuff: clear eyes and nose, full quills and fur, no bumps or sores. Watch him walk and run. He is naturally plump so don't consider a skinny one.

The hedgehog's natural defense is to roll into a tight ball and extend his quills. The first few times you might want to use some light leather gardening gloves to pick him up. He will learn to recognize you later on, and you can then slide your hand under his stomach and lift him gently. I suggest that you always keep him near a soft surface when holding him because he is unpredictable and will bite. You might react by dropping him or flinging him across the room. Neither would be good for the hedgehog!

Cage and Habitat Materials

The 10-gallon aquarium as shown in Fig. 16 will make the perfect hedgehog habitat. Fill to a depth of three inches with pine shavings. I must caution here that the jury is still out on cedar chips because of the fumes given off when cedar gets wet. Therefore, DON'T take a chance! Pine shavings can be purchased at the grocery store or, more expensively, at the pet shop. The breeders are developing and marketing new substrates on a daily basis so use your best judgement.

Hedgehogs sleep a lot, and I find that the best bedroom is a lunch-size brown paper bag. When this becomes torn or dirty, it is an easy thing to replace. A secure top is necessary. The hedgehog is a good climber and will climb up his water bottle, push up the lid, and bye-bye! It is a good idea to put a brick or other heavy object on the top.

Temperature/Light/Humidity

In the wild the hedgehog will sleep in its burrow to avoid the heat of the day. It is important not to over-heat the aquarium. The ideal temperature is about 70 degrees Fahrenheit. Keep the habitat away from the air-conditioning vents to avoid drafts and extremes in temperature. The humidity and light levels in the home or classroom are acceptable.

Food and Water

A basic diet of dry dog or cat food should be supplemented with chopped fruits and vegetables and a few mealworms at each meal. I keep the dry food, in small amounts, available at all times and give the worms, fruit, and vegetables once each day. Fresh water must be offered at all times and may be supplied by a small mammal water bottle that hangs on the inside of the aquarium.

Maintenance

As with all animals in captivity, cleanliness is best. Remove uneaten food daily. Dip feces out of the litter as they occur. The entire habitat should be dismantled and cleaned at least once each week. Use a mild dish soap to scrub the inside and then rinse thoroughly. Replace litter and hide-sack weekly.

Release or Disposal

The hedgehog will not survive in the city park! Call a local nature center for advice. Most zoos will not take them, but they may have someone to call. Call your local school and ask if a teacher would like to keep one as a classroom pet.

Notes and Afterthoughts

The pet store bookshelves are loaded with information about hedgehogs. Do your homework before you buy the animal and take it home!

Mice

Mice are very enjoyable pets for classroom or bedroom. They are one of what I call "fun to watch" pets. When given the proper apparatus, they can give you and your child many hours of pleasurable observation. They are the clowns of the animal world.

Acquisition and Handling

Mice can be purchased at almost any pet shop. Always look for healthy animals that are lively and move about the cage rapidly. Healthy mice are very inquisitive and have their nose in just about everything. They should have full fur, bright eyes, and clean pink tails. In all my years of having mice in the area, it always seems to me that mice will bite adults, but don't ever seem to bite children. The way I pick them up is to grasp them firmly by the tail and then lay them across my hand. They may feel threatened by being grabbed on the sides. Some lab personnel use the nape of the neck grasp, which is not recommended.

Cage and Habitat Materials

The best all-around habitat for one mouse or ten mice is the 10-gallon aquarium with a wire top as shown in Fig. 16. The litter should be cedar shavings or aspen shavings. I have also had some success with ground corn cob. This should be placed in the aquarium to a depth of at least three inches. The habitat can be decorated with a number of toys; the most successful I think are the paper rolls found in bathroom tissue and kitchen paper towels. You may also use shoe boxes or any other type of cardboard structure. I do not recommend buying an exercise wheel that you see in pet shops for gerbils or mice. These are dangerous for your pet; sometimes when they are moving around rapidly, the mouse will get caught and hurt himself.

Temperature/Light/Humidity

Mice are comfortable in room temperature surroundings and available light. The humidity will be sufficient if the top of the aquarium is not closed off too much. You should never lay a newspaper, book, or anything else on top of the aquarium. Humidity can be very detrimental to a mouse. Excess heat will kill a mouse faster than cold, so avoid it.

Food and Water

The rat block, a commercial product which is sold in all pet shops and a lot of grocery stores, is the best all-around diet for mice. This food may be supplemented by any number of food items from fresh vegetables, seeds, nuts, whole grains, and hay. Water should be provided at all times by using a pet waterer with a bracket that allows you to hang it from the inside of the aquarium.

Maintenance

Mice will usually urinate and defecate in one corner. This corner should be dipped out every third or fourth day. After a period of two to three weeks, the entire habitat should be dismantled and the aquarium cleaned with a mild dishwashing soap. The litter should be completely changed and you should replace the cardboard apparatus you have supplied.

Food should be offered in small amounts, and uneaten food should be removed at the end of the day to avoid spoilage.

Release and Disposal

When the mouse colony gets out of hand or you simply cannot handle them any longer, you might check with the pet shop from which you purchased them and they will sometimes take them back. You might also call your favorite teacher and ask if she would like some nice classroom pets that could also eventually be adopted.

Notes and Afterthoughts

If you want to purchase more than one mouse, I would suggest that you get females that are litter mates. Otherwise, you will have fighting or reproduction at an alarming rate. If you do plan to raise mice, you should be sure to have an outlet for your excess animals.

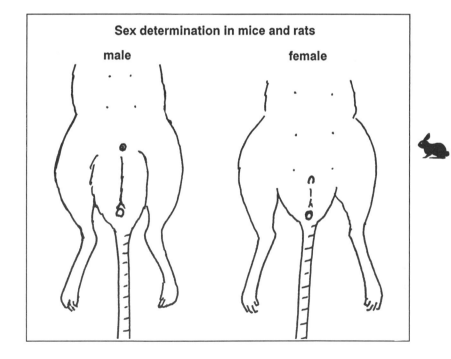

Rabbits

Ah, yes rabbits! They come in all sizes and dispositions and all make good pets. They can be trained to answer to their names, beg for food, signal to go out, to come in, and to use a litter box. They live between five and eight years. They must be kept clean!

Acquisition and Handling

Reputable pet shops are the best source. The dwarf variety of rabbits are small and require less space, but they are more hyperactive and tend to scratch and bite. The larger mongrel types are more laid back and easier to train. Check for muscle tone, clear eyes, dry pink nose, and clean ears (inside). They are best picked up by the scruff of the neck with one hand; then place the other hand beneath the rump. Do not pick up a rabbit by the ears! When holding a rabbit, be firm but gentle and be prepared for a sudden leap. The fall to the floor can cause serious injury.

Cage and Habitat Materials

Most rabbits can be happy in at least a two-foot-square cage. It would be cheaper if you build your own using the materials shown in Fig. 18. The cage should be placed in an area free of drafts and never in direct sunlight. The cage should have a wire-screen bottom to allow the feces to fall through. The tray beneath the cage should be covered with many layers of newspaper or at least one inch of cedar shavings or wood chips.

Food and Water

The rabbit pellets are the basic food but should be supplemented to maintain a healthy pet. Hay is needed as roughage and alfalfa is the best. The following can be offered in small amounts: whole oats, cracked corn, dried whole wheat bread also various grasses and greens and fresh vegetables. Wash the veggies first to remove chemical contamination. Feed small amounts. A salt lick mounted inside the cage will help prevent any mineral deficiencies. A water bottle should be available at all times.

Maintenance

The rabbit habitat must be cleaned every day as unhealthy conditions can build up overnight. Fresh food should be offered daily and uneaten food should be removed.

Release and Disposal

There could be a problem here. Keep in mind they live a long time so remember that before a commitment is made.

Should your situation change, first try friends and relatives. You might also contact one of your child's teachers for possible openings as a classroom pet. Rabbit breeders are always looking for new stock, and that might be an option.

Notes and Afterthoughts

A single female does best as a pet. They don't need rabies or distemper shots.

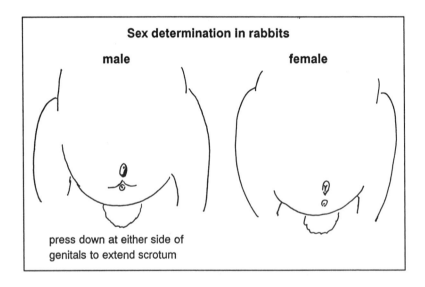

Sex determination in rabbits

male   female

press down at either side of genitals to extend scrotum

Rats

The word rat brings immediate disgust to parent and teacher alike. Adults take heart! The rat is the most intelligent, well-behaved, and cleanest of all the rodents we've talked about.

Acquisition and Handling

Rats can be acquired at almost any pet shop. Check the animal carefully to assure health by looking for a smooth shiny coat, dry on both ends, clear eyes, proper length of teeth, and general healthy appearance. A healthy rat is inquisitive and very active. As you get to know your rat, you will find that he can be picked up in just about any manner. It is best to introduce your hand so as to get your rat's attention before you pick him up. A frightened rat can be a little testy. Personally, I like the tail pick-up method and then lay the animal across the palm of my hand.

Cage and Habitat Materials

The best habitat for one rat is the 10-gallon aquarium with a wire top as shown in Fig. 16. The litter may be cedar or pine shavings, or you might use ground corn cob to a depth of at least three inches. Toys are a welcome diversion; keep in mind most everything edible will be eaten. Shoe boxes, toilet paper rolls, and old tennis shoes make wonderful playthings.

Temperature/Light/Humidity

Rats do well at room temperature with available light and humidity. Be careful not to close off the top of the aquarium with things such as magazines, newspapers, or books. Excess heat will kill a rat faster than cold, so be careful.

Food and Water

The rat block, which is sold in pet shops under a variety of names, is the best all-around diet for rats. This food may be supplemented by any number of food items to include fresh vegetables, seeds, nuts, whole grains, and hay. Water should be provided at all times by using a pet waterer bottle with a bracket that allows you to hang it from the inside of the aquarium.

Maintenance

A good rule of thumb is to clean as needed, which is usually once or twice a week. Food should be offered in small amounts, and all uneaten food should be removed at the end of the day to avoid spoilage. After a period of two to three weeks, the entire habitat should be dismantled and cleaned with a mild dishwashing soap, then rinsed thoroughly.

Release and Disposal

Check with these people in this order: neighbors, teachers, college science departments, then pet shops. Do not ever release a domestic rat into the wild.

Notes and Afterthoughts

To avoid fights, keep only litter mates or same-sex rats. If you do anticipate any population growth, be sure you first have an outlet for your excess animals. Pet shop people sometimes will tell you a rat is the sex you request just to make a sale. See the diagram on page 169 before you go shopping.

Sugar Gliders

The sugar glider is a small, flying squirrel-like marsupial that is native to Australia. He is a totally nocturnal, shy, nervous creature. The bookshelves are crowded with information about the care and keeping of these odd little mammals. None of them list the problems you might have. My instructions will assume that, for whatever reason, you have become the owner of a sugar glider. If you decide to continue the relationship, I hope you will read as much as you can find!

Acquisition and Handling

If you must buy one be sure you go to the trouble to find a breeder. Look those up in any pet related magazine. Better yet, check your newspaper classified section and give a home to one that is already suffering from neglect. Check for the usual things like bright eyes and a muscular build. He should be active, and if there is any question about his health, don't buy! Try for a baby, captive bred. Take great care to be gentle when handling your pet. They do not like to be constricted so cupped hands are best. They can and will bite. Although they are "gliders" they have difficulty catching air under the skin between their front and back legs when they are dropped or flung against a wall.

Cage and Habitat Materials

The cage should be made of wire, like the one in Fig. 18. The smallest cage for a pair of gliders should be 20" x 20" x 20". The taller the cage the better as they are tree dwellers and climbers. There should be many branches in the cage and the ultimate would be from a live fruit tree. Wild apple or sassafras are great but oak will do. They have rodent-like teeth and a need to gnaw. DO NOT USE ANY BRANCH THAT HAS BEEN SPRAYED WITH PESTICIDE. They must have a nesting box for hiding and sleep. You can buy a finch nesting box at any pet shop. Ground corn cob bedding seems to work best. Newsprint is OK but use old paper because the fresh ink can be harmful to your pet.

Temperature/Light/Humidity

If you can stand it, so can they! Room temperature and humidity will be just fine. Do not place the cage in front of an air-conditioning vent or in direct sunlight.

Food and Water

Gliders need lots of fruit and a little protein, so here is a partial list of food items: pineapple, peaches, apples, pears, strawberries, cantaloupe or other melon, grapes, oranges, corn, carrots, mealworms, peanuts, raisins. Feed them at about the same time daily. Use a shallow bowl. Water must be present at all times and can be provided by a small mammal water bottle that will hang on the outside of the cage.

Maintenance

Change litter when soiled. Put in new branches when the old ones become thoroughly gnawed. Remove uneaten food daily. Change and clean the water bottle daily.

Release or Disposal

The sugar glider should not be released into the wild. Call your local zoo or nature center for the names of animal rehabilitation specialists in your area. They usually have contacts with people who will give the animal perpetual care. When you relocate the animal consider whether or not he will at least get the care you gave or maybe even better.

Notes and Afterthoughts

Never put the cage in direct sunlight. Always check the cage door latch because they are escape artists. The sugar glider is a social animal and is happy in a crowd so get at least two. It is not a good idea to mix pets. Sugar gliders always stay in trees so they have no fear of dogs or cats. Getting them together may have disastrous results.

Chapter 9
SNAKES

Scaly, legless, sometimes venomous reptiles of the suborder Serpentes, having a long, tapering, cylindrical body.

Boa Constrictors

Boa constrictors are large tropical snakes that suffocate their prey by constriction. They are sold in pet shops when they are small, two to three feet, and you are usually not informed that they live twenty years and grow to ten feet! Size and legality aside, they do make desirable pets.

Acquisition and Handling

Boas may be purchased at a pet shop or from an individual usually through a newspaper ad. Purchasing from a dealer encourages collection from the wild.

It is difficult to generalize about handling boas. Factors such as time of day, hunger, and individual snake disposition can determine bite or not bite. They are more likely to strike while still in their cage. I use a distraction such as a cloth or piece of paper over its eyes and then pick up as much body as I can. While you are holding, support the snake's body as much as possible. Don't grasp and hold but allow free movement; just keep up with him.

Cage and Habitat Materials

The snake aquarium, Fig. 4, with the sliding pegboard top will best suit your snake. Size of snake will determine the size of aquarium: example two to four feet will fit a 10-gallon size; four to six feet, 20-gallon; six to nine feet, 55-gallon or larger. A hide box is necessary for security (see Fig. 20).

Old newspaper is the easiest floor cover. Boas are climbers so they need a branch. Be sure the branch is firmly placed so that it won't fall. If you are into appearances, you can use gravel, shavings, or bark chips. Be careful when feeding if you use shavings because he may ingest some. It is best to remove the snake from this substrate before feeding.

Temperature/Light/Humidity

The warm end of the habitat should be maintained at 80 to 85 degrees Fahrenheit (see Fig. 7, Fig. 8, Fig. 10, and Fig. 11). Available light will suffice. Humidity should be just shy of condensation on the glass. Humidity can be regulated by the size of the water bowl.

Food and Water

Boas eat warm-blooded prey. Feeding live prey is not necessary and is unwise because the prey might bite and injure the snake. Mice, rats, and small chickens can be frozen and thawed as needed. Depending on the size of the snake, feed the appropriate-size food item about once each week. If for some reason they refuse food, you can just refreeze and try again later. Refer to the chapter on Sick Call for snake feeding methods.

The water bowl should be large enough for the snake to immerse in completely if he wants. Do not allow him to soak for more than 24 hours as this may cause blisters. Put a rock in the bowl leaving just enough room for him to drink.

Maintenance

Change substrate (floor cover) at least once each week. Wash and dry the inside of the cage using Lysol or Rocal D solution. Change water daily. Do not leave food items on the cage floor more than a few hours.

Release and Disposal

They cannot be released unless you take them to South America. Try to find someone who will give him the proper cage and care. Contact the biology department of a university or your local zoo reptile department and ask for the nearest herpetological society location.

Notes and Afterthoughts

Be sure the food item is completely thawed and warm. Offer food with kitchen tongs or long forceps as they are bad shots and may miss the first time and get your hand! You should not handle your boa for at least 24 hours after he has eaten. Sometimes handling them makes them regurgitate.

Bullsnakes

Bullsnakes are large as North American snakes go. They may grow to over six feet. They are wonderful bluffers and will puff up and blow air through their mouths and make a loud hissing sound. Soon after they are caught, this behavior subsides.

Momma bullsnake lays five to ten white, leathery eggs in early summer. The newborns are full of bull and ready to go from day one. They are constrictors and eat small rodents, birds, and bird eggs.

Acquisition and Handling

Bullsnakes can be field collected. They like to hide beneath boards and pieces of tin found around abandoned barns and old houses. If picked up quickly, they usually do not try to bite.

When handling, support as much of their bodies as possible. It is not necessary to hold them behind the head. Hold them loosely and do not try to prevent their movement as this might cause them to bite.

Cage and Habitat Materials

Depending upon the size of the snake, a 10- or 20-gallon aquarium will make an excellent cage. A sliding top (illustration in Fig. 4) is necessary as they are great escape artists. I prefer several layers of old newspaper cut to cover the bottom of the aquarium. You may use gravel, bark chips, or aspen chips. Care should be used when feeding, because they may ingest particles or rocks. A hiding box should be provided (see Fig. 20).

Temperature/Light/Humidity

The habitat should be maintained at between 78 degrees and 85 degrees Fahrenheit. A warm end and a cool end of the habitat may be created by putting a light at one end of the aquarium as shown in the illustration in Fig. 11. Allowing the habitat to become too dry or too wet may cause health problems. Ordinarily, the watering bowl will supply enough humidity for your particular aquarium. Too much humidity will show up as condensation on the glass and you should use a smaller water bowl in that case. If it is too dry, he may have trouble shedding his skin.

Food and Water

Bullsnakes eat warm-blooded prey. It will be necessary to feed them mice and small rats. These may be kept frozen and simply thawed when it is time to eat. Be sure the food item is completely thawed, as an ice ball in his stomach will certainly cause the snake problems. Bullsnakes will also eat warm chicken eggs. It is an educational experience to watch them do that. Water can be provided with a heavy, flat water bowl, much like the ceramic bowls used for large dogs.

Maintenance

The entire habitat should be dismantled and thoroughly cleaned weekly and more often if needed. The water bowl should be cleaned and filled daily. Use a mild dish soap to clean and be sure to rinse thoroughly.

Release and Disposal

The animal may be released where he was caught. If this location is not known, consult your reference books for a geographic range. They hibernate, so release them during the warm months.

Notes and Afterthoughts

Bullsnakes are apt to bite when they are about to shed. This is indicated by a clouded appearance of the skin and foggy eyes. They may also be prone to bite just before or just after they have eaten. When feeding a thawed mice to your snake, simply dangle it by the tail in front of the snake. Be cautious, as bullsnakes are not great shots; he may miss and get you in the hand!

CAUTION: Do not pursue or capture an unidentified snake.

Cornsnakes

Cornsnakes make wonderful part-time pets. They are also called red ratsnakes. The belly is beautifully checkered with black on white; the top is a pretty red or orange with a considerable color variation among individuals. They are found from southern New Jersey to southern Florida, and west to Louisiana. They grow to a length of from 30 to 48 inches.

Acquisition and Handling

The cornsnakes are farm and field animals and can be found near their food source, which is mice, rats, and small rabbits. They are most often beneath man's garbage, such as boards, pieces of tin, old mattresses, and other junkyard goodies.

I use the flat hand capture method. This tactic means that when you identify the snake on the ground, quickly place a flat hand over his head and press firmly. You then manipulate the head between your index finger and your thumb. Or if you don't mind being bitten, just grab him! When he is in the aquarium, it is best to introduce your hand and get the snake's attention before you pick him up. Support as much of the snake's body as is possible, because they are prone to back injuries. Allow the snake to move loosely through your grasp and try not to be too restrictive.

Cage and Habitat Materials

The good ol' 10-gallon aquarium with the sliding pegboard top as seen in Fig. 4 is the best habitat. Multi-layers of newspaper cut to fit the aquarium are an inexpensive and easily maintained substrate. You may also use gravel, fresh bark, and I hesitate to say, aspen shavings, because they are sometimes eaten along with the food items. Do not use cedar chips because when they get wet, they give off an obnoxious odor and the fumes may cause breathing problems in your captive. Provide a hide box like the ones shown in Fig. 20.

Temperature/Light/Humidity

Cornsnakes do well in room temperature and room light. Keep in mind they are reptiles, and when they are cool, they become lethargic and may not eat. Humidity can be regulated by the size and surface area of the water dish. If the snake turns the water dish over, change the paper as soon as possible because excess moisture can cause skin problems. If the humidity is too low, the effects will be noticed in the dry appearance of the snake's skin. Be careful not to place the habitat too near to an air conditioning vent as he may get too hot or too cold. If the room temperature falls below 65 degrees Fahrenheit, you should arrange a heat source as illustrated in Fig. 7, Fig. 8, or Fig. 11. As with other snakes, the cornsnake needs a warm end of the habitat as well as a cool end. This will allow him to seek his optimum temperature.

Food and Water

Cornsnakes will easily take thawed-out frozen mice dangled in front of their nose. Be sure the mouse is completely thawed and warm before you offer it to the snake. Water should be provided in a heavy, flat-bottomed dish, and you should place a rock in the middle of the dish to prevent the animal from oversoaking. A good maintenance diet is one adult mouse per week.

Maintenance

The entire habitat should be dismantled and completely cleaned at least once a week and more often if necessary. Use a mild dishwashing soap, rinse thoroughly, and dry with a paper towel. The water dish should be cleaned and refilled daily.

Release and Disposal

Be sure you are within the geographic range of this animal before he is released. It is best to release him in the spring months so he can readjust, reacclimate, and prepare for winter, during which he will hibernate.

Notes and Afterthoughts

I have said it before, and I'll say it again. Never feed any snake live food because the prey animal may bite the snake.

CAUTION: Do not pursue or capture an unidentified snake.

Garter Snakes

There are a number of different species, all of which are nonvenomous and very similar in appearance and behavior. They range in size from eighteen to thirty inches and are about one quarter inch in diameter and can be found from Canada to South America. The natural habitat is marshy, wet pastureland or meadows. Their primary food in the wild is earthworms, frogs, and small toads and fish if they can catch them.

Acquisition and Handling

They can be found in the field or bought from a pet shop. To pick up a garter snake, move slowly towards it and pick up as much of the body as you can while remaining quiet and calm. They sometimes bite when picked up, but generally they will only emit a foul-smelling musk and bump their snouts against your hand. They do have sharp little

teeth, so if he grabs you, try to avoid causing an airborne snake!

Cage and Habitat Materials

An escape-proof cage is essential if you don't want a loose snake in your house or classroom, as they can slip through the smallest crack. The most suitable cage is a 10-gallon aquarium with a sliding pegboard top. See the illustration in Fig. 4. The easiest substrate for the aquarium is old newspaper cut to fit. You can decorate the interior using aquarium gravel, logs, and rocks for appearance. Secure the top with a screw or nail through the pegboard (file off the point).

Temperature/Light/Humidity

They do not require extra heat and will do well in normal room temperature and artificial light or filtered sunlight. A large water bowl will supply the needed humidity and a place to swim.

Food and Water

Feed live goldfish, minnows, and large guppies by placing them in the water bowl. You can also feed them small frogs and toads. These do not have to be live, however. Using a pair of forceps, dangle the frog or toad in front of the snake's nose. A water bowl large enough for the snake to immerse himself should be provided. Feed two food items per week.

Maintenance

About once a week remove all habitat material and clean the aquarium thoroughly with soap and water. Rinse well and dry.

Release and Disposal

More than likely the snake can be released locally. Be sure and release the snake in an isolated area where there is little chance of it encountering a human. Preferably, release him near a water source. They do hibernate, so release them during the warm months.

Notes and Afterthoughts

Don't forget the fish in the water bowl. Remove them at the end of the day.

CAUTION: Do not pursue or capture an unidentified snake.

Hog-nose Snakes

Depending upon your area of the country, these animals are referred to as puff adders or spreading adders. Hog-nose snakes are harmless animals. They are rather unique in a number of ways. First of all, they are very species-specific in what they eat. They dine primarily on toads. They paralyze them by using a mildly venomous saliva and swallow them whole, much as the constrictors do. Second, they have a curious defense mechanism; hog-nose snakes actually play dead. When the going gets rough, they will lay on their backs and roll their tongue out to one side and appear to be dead. As soon as the danger passes, they will roll back on their stomachs and slither away. One strange thing about this activity is that while they are on their backs playing dead, if you roll them over on their stomachs, they will immediately roll back over on their backs as if they know that a dead snake is supposed to be upside down!

Acquisition and Handling

The hog-nose snake is one of those that might come in with a student or a child in a paper bag or a can. We have built our habitats over the hog-nose habitat; consequently, they can be found in parks, picnic areas, backyards, flower beds, and other places inhabited by people. Upon being approached, a hog-nose snake, true to his other names, will flatten his body and hiss and strike violently. He has much the same appearance as a frightened cobra. I have found that even if they strike, their mouths hit your hand closed in an effort just to scare you away. If grabbed and picked up, although they might not bite, they have an obnoxious habit of musking. They emit a very foul-smelling musk from the anal opening at the rear of their tail.

Habitat

A 10-gallon aquarium with a sliding top as illustrated in Fig. 4 is an excellent habitat for any of the hog-nose snakes we have here in the United States. For the cage bottom, I prefer the cut newspaper — several layers are needed, but you can use gravel or aspen shavings or crushed bark chips. You must be careful when using these other substrates, because when the snakes eat, they have a tendency to take in particles which may cause intestinal blockages. They should be provided with a hiding box, like those illustrated in Fig. 20. You may decorate as you wish, although as with most habitat decorations, it is more for human esthetics than snake requirements.

Temperature/Light/Humidity

Aquarium temperature should be somewhere between 70 and 80 degrees Fahrenheit. Room light is sufficient and humidity can be regulated by the size of the watering bowl. The humidity should not be too high, as indicated by condensation on the side of the aquarium walls; nor should it be too dry, which can be noticed in the snake's general skin appearance.

Food and Water

Of the two species of hog-nose snakes in North America, the most common is the Eastern hog-nose, and it is the most difficult to feed because it eats almost exclusively toads. If there is not a ready supply of toads available, there is a trick you can try. The hog-nose uses his sense of smell primarily to locate food items. You might take a thawed mouse and rub it briskly against the skin of a toad. The scent is transferred and the snake might take the mouse. If not, you might be prepared to keep your hog-nose for a short period of time and then release him. Water can be provided in a heavy, shallow dish. You might also place a rock in the center of the dish so that the snake cannot coil in the water and soak too long. Soaking sometimes causes skin problems.

Maintenance

It will be necessary to dismantle and completely clean the aquarium at least once a week and more often if needed. The hiding box should be cleaned or replaced and the interior of the aquarium cleaned with a mild dishwashing soap and rinsed thoroughly and dried. The water bowl should be emptied, cleaned, and filled daily.

Release and Disposal

Your hog-nose snake should be released in the area where it was collected. If that is not possible, check your reference books for appropriate geographic locations and release in an area as close to that as possible. It is best to release the animal in the spring months so he may readjust and reestablish himself before the winter months when it is time to hibernate.

Notes and Afterthoughts

When all else fails with food offers, try a live grass frog.

CAUTION: Do not pursue or capture an unidentified snake.

Lined Snakes

Lined snakes are from six to seven inches long and have a diameter about the size of a pencil. They have dark green and light yellow stripes running down their backs. Their stomachs are light yellow with black dots on each belly scale, forming two lines from head to tail.

Since the lined snake is not poisonous, it is not necessary to call the police to shoot a live one or to balance a dead one on a leaf rake all the way from the front yard to the garbage can out back. They are really a garden asset because they eat crickets and other bugs that harm your plants. These snakes are more commonly known as garden snakes, grass snakes, or garter snakes. They stay hidden during the day and come out at night to hunt for food. They do not usually bite but will emit a foul-smelling odor if molested.

Acquisition and Handling

The lined snake prefers areas beneath garden stones, bricks, old wood piles, and inside the hole with your water meter. They can be picked up gently, being careful to support as much of their bodies as possible. You will need to wash your hands when you are through handling them because of the musk they produce.

Cage and Habitat Materials

The ideal container for these small snakes is a wide-mouthed gallon jar, with holes punched in the lid, filled to about three inches with aquarium gravel or pea gravel. See setup in Fig. 6. Place small flat pieces of bark or thin rocks in your container to supply hiding places.

Temperature/Lighting/Humidity

They do well at room temperature. Be careful not to place the jar near a heat source such as a window or heating vent. Room light is sufficient. Spray the gravel with water occasionally (twice a week) to prevent your captive from becoming snake-jerky.

Food and Water

Preferred food for these animals is earthworms. They will also eat small insects such as crickets, grasshoppers, roaches, or mealworms that can be purchased at your pet shop. You can catch your own with the trap shown in Fig. 3. Feed an average of one insect per day. Sink a small baby food jar in the gravel; fill with marbles or marble-sized pebbles and add water. This prevents the snake from soaking too long and causing skin problems.

Maintenance

Always remove uneaten food at the end of each day. Change water and clean out the water jar as needed. Clean and rinse the entire habitat at least every two weeks. Use a mild detergent and rinse thoroughly.

Release and Disposal

Try to release the animal pretty close to where you found him and about the same time of year. These animals should not be kept for more than one year as they may suffer from malnutrition.

Notes and Afterthoughts

Be careful about the size differential between insect prey and snake. A good rule of thumb is that if the insect is bigger than the snake's head, do not give it to him.

CAUTION: Do not pursue or capture an unidentified snake.

Prairie Kingsnakes

Prairie kingsnakes range throughout the south central United States from southern Iowa to southern Texas. The adults are between thirty and forty-two inches long. They are dark snakes with colors of brown, red, and green. Their bellies are yellowish with squarish brown blotches. They are residents of grassland prairies, open woodlands, and meadows.

Acquisition and Handling

These snakes can be easily caught throughout the spring in their native habitat. The best hiding places are under large flat stones and human debris such as boards, pieces of cardboard, tin, and trash piles. They turn up regularly in pet shops, but you should not waste your money.

They will associate anything that comes through the top of the aquarium with food so introduce your hand slowly. Support as much of their bodies as possible and allow them to slip freely through your hands. After your first bite from these snakes, you are considered a kingsnake expert and you can grab him anywhere you can! Otherwise, a flat hand over the head and then grasp on either side besides the jaws will control him nicely. Cradle as much of his body with the other hand as possible. They have a nasty habit of defecating when immobilized, so you might try to aim the tail portion appropriately!

Cage and Habitat Materials

The basic snake cage is diagrammed in Fig. 4. The substrate material can be sand or gravel. I use about five layers of newsprint for all my snakes. Natural habitat decorations are really for the observer and not necessary for the snake's well-being. They do require a hide box for security. This can be made from a plastic butter dish with lid and a hole of appropriate diameter cut in the side as shown in Fig. 20.

Temperature/Light/Humidity

The optimum temperature for this snake is between 78 and 85 degrees Fahrenheit. This may be accomplished by using a hot rock, diagramed in Fig. 7, or a heat lamp as seen in Fig. 8, or Fig. 11. Room lighting is sufficient unless you are planning to attempt breeding, and that's the subject of another book! Humidity is provided by the evaporation from the water bowl.

Food and Water

Prairie kingsnakes do nicely on one dead mouse each week. They are really cannibals, but I do not recommend feeding him other snakes! Mice may be bought and stored in your freezer. Before feeding, be sure that the mouse is thawed thoroughly and even a little warm. Dangle the mouse by the tail in front of the snake's nose, and he will take it immediately if he is hungry. He may not eat if the temperature is too low or he is about to shed his skin. A water bowl of a not-too-easy-to-turn-over type should be provided. Do not allow the snake to soak in the bowl for more than a few hours at a time as he will develop skin problems. To avoid prolonged soaking, fill the bowl with small stones or marbles and that will allow him to drink and not soak.

Maintenance

Remove soiled substrate as soon as the feces dries. Dismantle and completely clean the habitat with a disinfectant. Rinse thoroughly as the snake may react to any residual odors or resins from the disinfectant. Change and clean the water bowl daily.

Release and Disposal

Try to release the animal as close to its place of origin as possible. Time of year is critical; i.e., don't turn him out in mid-winter.

Notes and Afterthoughts

Prairie kingsnakes, just like all snakes, are escape artists. The slightest crack left in the sliding door will be found and utilized. The resulting searches and explanations to relatives and friends will prove mind-boggling! If he happens to get loose in the house or classroom, you just have to search, wait, and watch. He will be found in the least likely place by the least likely person! The person who is most afraid of him is going to find him!

CAUTION: Do not pursue or capture an unidentified snake.

Pythons

There are many, many different species of pythons that are available in pet shops; therefore, I will make this entry as general as is necessary to get the job done. The most common python on the market is the Burmese python. When purchased, it may be no longer than eighteen to twenty-four inches long. In five to ten years it may grow to a length of fifteen feet and weigh over 100 pounds. This is a primary consideration when obtaining one of these animals. There is also a popular animal called the Ball python; these reach a length of two to three feet. Although they are very shy and it is difficult to get them to eat, they are more desirable simply because of their size. These snakes are constrictors and occasionally size will make this a very primary consideration, not necessarily for the owner, but for those who do not know much about snakes. They do squeeze and suffocate their prey but are not prone or known to eat people.

Acquisition and Handling

These snakes may be purchased from pet shops where they are legally sold. I would suggest you consult your local newspaper ads. These animals are usually purchased by someone who does not know much about snakes, and as soon as they are bitten or the snake gets quite large, they begin looking for homes. You can usually pick up a snake plus the cage at a very reasonable price. I found that most giant snakes and most other snakes are prone to bite when they are in their habitat. I have found it to my advantage to distract the snakes before picking them up. I use a piece of clothing or newspaper to cover the snake's head and then I quickly grab as much body as I can and remove the animal from the cage. Each individual snake has its own personality, and after a while, you will learn when to grab and when not to grab. Although the bite can be painful, the teeth are short and needle-like and usually only scratches or small puncture wounds will occur.

Cage and Habitat Materials

Depending upon the size when you get it, the habitat will range from a small sweater box with holes to hundreds of gallons worth of aquarium space! The top enclosing device is the most important item in your habitat setup. All of these snakes are escape artists and will leave at any opportunity that presents itself. The sliding pegboard top as shown in Fig. 4 is the most escape-proof lid I have ever used. The habitat can be decorated to the desire of the owner. I have found that snakes require nothing more than a few layers of old newspaper and perhaps a limb for climbing and stretching.

Temperature/Light/Humidity

These factors are critical to the well-being of the python. The temperature should be maintained between 75 and 85 degrees Fahrenheit, leaning towards the upper end of that range. Heat may be provided in a number of ways: the heat rock shown in Fig. 7, the incandescent bulb in the jar as shown in Fig. 10, or the gooseneck lamp at the end of the aquarium as illustrated in Fig. 11. These may be used singly or in combination depending upon how much heat is necessary. The heat should be provided so that the animal may move from a warmer part of the habitat to a cooler part of the habitat. The light cycle is not of importance in these particular species unless you are breeding snakes, and that is the subject of a whole new book! The habitat can become too dry or too moist; both situations can cause health problems. Avoid having a wet habitat — usually room humidity will be sufficient. The water bowl will provide the needed moisture.

Food and Water

Snakes drink a lot more water than most people think. An ample supply of water should be provided at all times. It is best to use a heavy ceramic dog dish that is difficult for the snake to overturn. He will try to do this almost every time! Pythons are primarily warm-blooded-animal eaters; food may be in the form of birds or mammals which should be fed warm and dead. Rats, guinea pigs, hamsters, rabbits, baby chicks, pigeons — all of these qualify for python food. This may be a consideration as to whether or not to house one of these animals, depending upon how you feel about the food material. They should never be fed a live food item as this might cause injury to your snake. Usually a dangled food item that is warm and moving will be taken readily. Most bites occur during the feeding process, so be careful not to expose your fingers or hand along with the food item. Although they are quite efficient hunters in the wild, in captivity they seem to have a very poor aim.

Maintenance

It is necessary to remove all fecal material and soiled litter as they occur. The water bowl should be removed, cleaned, and refilled daily. The entire habitat should be dismantled and cleaned thoroughly with a mild dishwashing detergent at least once a week.

Release and Disposal

You cannot release a python in the United States. Therefore, it will be necessary to contact various people, beginning with the local zoo. They will probably refuse the animal but may have some other resources, such as the local herpetological society or a private collector, who would be happy to give your animal a home. You might also call nature centers in the area, or check with school teachers in your biology department. They may want to use it as a classroom study animal.

Notes and Afterthoughts

Check the local city ordinances about keeping snakes in the home. They may be illegal.

CAUTION: Do not pursue or capture an unidentified snake.

Ratsnakes

Ratsnakes are probably the most common constrictors found in North America. There are several different species. Some of those by common name would be the Texas ratsnake, the Trans-Pecos ratsnake, the black ratsnake, and others. The husbandry is similar in all these snakes. All are constrictors, which simply means they suffocate their prey by wrapping coils around its body. In the wild, they eat warm-blooded animals, such as small birds, and various rodents, such as rats, mice, and others. Ratsnakes will also eat eggs; they are sometimes called chicken snakes depending upon the region in which they are found. They are quite large and can grow to lengths of over six feet. They are somewhat characteristically nippy. They make wonderful classroom and home pets for behavior observation but are not much on being handled.

Acquisition and Handling

Ratsnakes inhabit farm and field and are found most often near their sources of food. This may be old out-buildings, stables, barns, places where there is a lot of debris in the area, and of course where there may be mice, small birds, and eggs. The slow approach is best used when handling a ratsnake. Let the snake know you are there before picking it up. Touch the snake a few times first and then gently move it a little bit. A slow approach will reduce the likelihood of startling the snake and lets it know it's going to be handled. If the snake is not comfortable, it will try to escape or attain a position where it feels it will be comfortable. Do not grasp the snake; just provide as much support as you can for its entire body. Allow him to move freely through your hands.

Cage and Habitat Materials

A 10-gallon aquarium with the sliding pegboard top is best for housing ratsnakes as shown in Fig. 4. The multi-layers of newspaper cut to fit the bottom of the aquarium is the best substrate for these animals. You may also use gravel, aspen shavings, or crushed bark to a depth of about one inch. Be careful when feeding as this material may be ingested and cause intestinal blockages. They like hide boxes and you can supply one as shown in Fig. 20.

Temperature/Light/Humidity

Ratsnakes can be easily maintained in room temperature and room light. Humidity can be regulated by the size and surface area of the water dish. If the humidity is too high, it will form condensation on the sides of the glass. If the humidity is too low, the effects will be noticed in the dry appearance of the snake's skin. Do not place the aquarium near an air conditioning vent, as it will be too chilly for him. If the room temperature falls below 65 degrees, it will be necessary to arrange a heat source, as illustrated in Fig. 8, Fig. 10, or Fig. 11. As with other snakes, it needs a warm end of the habitat and a cool end of the habitat.

Food and Water

Ratsnakes readily accept thawed-out frozen mice by dangling them in front of their noses. Water should be provided in a heavy, flat-bottomed dish, and you should place a rock in the middle of the bowl to prevent the snake from oversoaking. Feed one mouse each week. You may try the same mouse more than once if he refuses the first time. Refrigerate the mouse and try again the next day.

Maintenance

You should dismantle and completely clean out the habitat at least once a week and more often if necessary. The aquarium should be cleaned with a mild dishwashing soap, rinsed thoroughly, and dried. Change and clean the water dish daily.

Release and Disposal

Sometimes these snakes are acquired from pet shops. It will be necessary to ascertain its exact identification and then check your references for release in the proper geographic location. It is best to release them in the spring months so they can readjust, reacclimate, and be prepared for the colder months in which they hibernate.

Notes and Afterthoughts

Never feed any snake live food. The reason behind this is that in the wild, when a snake attacks its prey, the prey sometimes attacks and bites the snake. A snake in the wild travels continuously and thereby keeps whatever wounds he gets from his prey clean and allows for proper healing. In a cage situation, the snake does not move constantly and, therefore, the wound may become infected and will certainly cause a problem.

CAUTION: Do not pursue or capture an unidentified snake.

Ring-necked Snakes

Ring-necked snakes, although not as impressive as the larger snakes, are very interesting pets and quite common. This is one of the snakes most likely to be found in the can or jar carried by a young child. This snake is earthworm-sized, a dark green or brown in color, and has a brilliantly colored yellow or red or orange neck band. They have brightly colored orange belly scales with black dots. An interesting defense mechanism these little snakes have is that, when frightened, they expose their underside of brilliant orange and curl the end of their tail and wiggle it. This, of course, is a diversion from the head of the animal, and most animals or predators will bite or nip the tail.

Acquisition and Handling

The ring-necked snake is common in many areas throughout the southeastern and south central United States and may be found under almost any shallow laying debris, such as boards, flat rocks, pieces of tin, etc. They do have musk glands to ward off predators. The ring-necked snake will initially musk when picked up, but this defensive action will lessen as he is handled more often.

Cage and Habitat Materials

The cage for this animal must be kept simple because they are burrowers, and if you construct an elaborate environmental chamber, you will never see the creature. I use a wide-mouthed gallon jar as shown in Fig. 6 in which I place a half-inch of aquarium gravel, a small flat rock, and perhaps a twig or two for decoration. In this situation, a plastic aquarium plant looks very nice and provides cover for your pet.

Temperature/Light/Humidity

These snakes can be maintained at room temperature. They do hibernate in the winter, so cold weather causes them to be inactive and they will burrow extensively. Room light is sufficient; they do prefer high humidity or moderate humidity. The habitat should be sprayed or misted occasionally.

Food and Water

Ring-necked snakes eat soft-bodied insects, such as caterpillars, but also consume worms and crickets. The crickets you use should be small, and I sometimes remove the jumping legs to allow for easier swallowing. The food should be offered every third day, and uneaten food should be removed at the end of the day.

Maintenance

Your gallon-jar habitat should be completely dismantled and cleaned with a mild dishwashing detergent at least once a week. All uneaten food and dried feces should be removed on a regular basis.

Release and Disposal

The animal should be released at or near the site where he was collected. If that is not possible, you should try to match the environmental conditions as closely as you can before releasing the animal. Do not release him in fall or winter, as this will most certainly cause his demise.

Notes and Afterthoughts

These little snakes will do their defensive act only for the first few encounters. Get your audience together before you tell them what should happen.

CAUTION: Do not pursue or capture an unidentified snake.

Rough-earth Snakes

These snakes are most commonly called ground snakes or garden snakes. Most people consider them babies when they are found because they are so small. Actually, they never get over ten inches long and are no bigger around than a pencil. They are a rather nondescript brown to tan snake, although some in certain areas attain many brilliant colors. They eat primarily worms and insects in the wild. They are rather difficult to maintain in captivity because when they are doing well, you don't see them since they are secretive and burrowers.

Acquisition and Handling

These small snakes can easily be found under garden bricks, log piles, and various other debris that are found in back-yards. You must be careful when handling these small animals as they are rather fragile. Not only do they not even try to bite, their mouths are not large enough to get a hold.

Cage and Habitat Materials

These small snakes will do well in a wide-mouthed glass jar filled to a depth of three inches with moist humus which should be covered to one-quarter inch with leaf mold. Small rotting logs and flat stones may also be introduced.

Temperature/Light/Humidity

These snakes can be maintained at room temperature with available light. They do require high humidity and this may be obtained by using a plant atomizer about once each day and simply spraying the leaf litter one or two times.

Food and Water

Feeding the rough-earth snake is somewhat difficult if you do not have source of insects or insect larvae. They love earthworms, which can be easily obtained at the local bait shop. They will also eat baby crickets and various grubs. They enjoy ant and termite eggs. Water can be supplied from a small baby food jar. Marbles or small stones should be placed in the jar so that the animals cannot oversoak and cause blisters.

Maintenance

When the habitat becomes moldy or excessively wet or the jar clouds with condensation, it will be necessary to change the substrate. Clean the jar thoroughly. Use a mild dishwashing liquid and rinse well.

Release and Disposal

Simply take the snake back out into the yard or garden and let him go. Do not release the animal during the cold months, as they do hibernate and they need time to prepare for it.

Notes and Afterthoughts

Although these snakes are easily cared for, as I mentioned, if things are going well, you will not see them in their habitat. Therefore, I would suggest that you keep them only for a short period of time.

CAUTION: Do not pursue or capture an unidentified snake.

Rough Green Tree Snakes

These pencil-thin, long green snakes are experts at camouflage. They hunt among the branches high in the trees and
at the first sign of danger, they freeze in place and become
almost invisible.

Acquisition and Handling

Tree snakes can be field collected with a practiced eye and
with a lot of luck. They are quick but usually do not
attempt to bite when seized. They should be supported as
much as possible when you are holding them.

Cage and Habitat Materials

A 10- or 20-gallon aquarium is enough space for a tree
snake. Tree snakes enjoy something tall with many
branches. Greenery can be supplied by inserting plastic
branches into holes drilled in a limb or log. Gravel or
crushed rock makes a good substrate. A screen cage top
may be used with this snake because they are not prone to
nose rubbing as some snakes are. A hide box is required on
the floor of the cage. See Fig. 20.

Temperature/Light/Humidity

These snakes do best in high humidity at temperatures
between 75 and 85 degrees Fahrenheit. Temperature may
be regulated by using any of the methods illustrated in Fig.
7, Fig. 8, Fig. 10, or Fig. 11. Room light is sufficient.

Food and Water

Green tree snakes are insect eaters. Crickets and grasshoppers are easily caught. Other insects such as moths can be
captured in the insect trap shown in Fig. 3. Offer these live
and only one or two at a time at least twice each week. A
large shallow water dish will supply sufficient humidity for
the cage.

Maintenance

The gravel or other substrate should be removed and washed as is needed. Remove dead or uneaten insects at the end of the day. Clean and fill water bowl daily. Dismantle the habitat and clean with a mild detergent about once each month.

Release and Disposal

Let him go where you found him. Release should be after the last freeze and long before the first frost of the year.

Notes and Afterthoughts

Rough green tree snakes are delicate and should be considered short-term captives.

CAUTION: Do not pursue or capture an unidentified snake.

Water Snakes

Water snakes are very common in temperate climates and there are a number of different species that inhabit all of our streams, ponds, and lakes. They get a bad reputation because, being in water, they automatically are taken for water moccasins. Although they are nonpoisonous, they are very aggressive snakes, and I would not recommend keeping an adult as a pet. The young snakes seem to do quite well for a short period of time.

Acquisition and Handling

Juvenile water snakes can be found near any body of water. It is easy to locate them by turning over rocks, boards, logs — anything near the water's edge. Be very careful when doing this because that habitat also harbors the poisonous water moccasin. Handling a small water snake is a simple matter of grabbing and holding on. They sometimes will coil and strike at anything that moves, but the teeth are not large enough to break the skin. They are a musking snake; when you pick them up they will spread a foul-smelling, yellowish-colored musk over your hand. After continuous handling this activity will cease.

Cage and Habitat Materials

Although water snakes do stay in or near water at all times, water is not absolutely necessary for their survival. Their habitat should contain a nice large water bowl so they can swim. The best habitat for a water snake is a 10-gallon aquarium; it can be decorated with gravel, rocks, small logs, and of course a large water bowl.

Temperature/Light/Humidity

Water snakes can be maintained at room temperature in available light. The humidity will be quite high because of the large water bowl, which is perfectly OK. The optimum habitat temperature of the water snake is between 75 and

85 degrees Fahrenheit. You can use any of the heating methods shown in Fig. 8, Fig. 10, or Fig. 11.

Food and Water

Water snakes thrive on small cricket frogs and can also be fed goldfish that you purchase at the pet shops. The goldfish can simply be released into the water bowl and the water snake will be more than happy to catch them for himself. He should be fed at least one or two food items per week.

Maintenance

The water snake's aquarium habitat should be dismantled and cleaned at least once each week. The water may become fouled if a food item dies or if a snake kills a food item and does not eat it right away. The water should be changed daily or as needed.

Release and Disposal

When water snakes reach a size of somewhere between a foot and a half to two feet they will become very aggressive, and their bite can be quite painful. They have needle-sharp teeth and they will bite you continuously as long as you hold on. They may be released in much the same area as you caught them or near any body of water. Release them during the warm months as they do hibernate.

Notes and Afterthoughts

The cage top for the water snake must necessarily be wire so as not to have the humidity level too high. Be careful that you use small enough wire so that the snake cannot get through and also that the edges are secure so he cannot push the top off. See the illustration in Fig. 23.

CAUTION: Do not pursue or capture an unidentified snake.

Chapter 10
TURTLES

Reptiles of the order Chelonia, having horny, toothless jaws and the body enclosed in a bony or leathery shell into which the head, limbs, and tail can be withdrawn in most species.

214 • Chapter 10

Box Turtles

There are many kinds of box turtles found in North America. The husbandry is basically the same for all of them. They live naturally in grassy areas, such as meadows and fields where the vegetation is abundant. The female lays her eggs in moist earth or decaying vegetation, and incubation occurs through natural heat.

Acquisition/Handling

They are easily obtained during the spring when they travel a lot searching for a mate. They can usually be picked up while crossing roads, especially after a gentle rain. They are sold in pet shops; but be careful, as they can really be stressed due to poor care and inadequate diet. Look for clear, open eyes, lots of foot movement, and body weight commensurate with size. Pick up the turtle by grasping the shell on either side from the top. Do not hold the turtle upside-down or place him on his back, as this is very uncomfortable and might cause health problems. Some species are characteristically nippy, so watch your fingers.

Cage and Habitat Materials

The best home for the box turtle is a 10-gallon aquarium. No top is needed unless you have a very inquisitive cat. The best substrate is eight to ten layers of old newspaper cut to fit the bottom of the aquarium. A small cardboard box may be provided for a hiding spot. Natural materials may be used that are more attractive, but they are harder to clean. Three inches of aquarium gravel with rocks and small logs is an attractive display. Plants, artificial or natural, will be quickly consumed or crushed.

Temperature/Light/Humidity

Box turtles need heat and sunlight to remain healthy. Heat may be provided by placing a lamp with a 25-watt bulb near one end of the aquarium as shown in Fig. 11. The temperature in the aquarium should not exceed 85 degrees, nor drop below 70 degrees Fahrenheit. Unfiltered sunlight is required so the animal can utilize vitamin intake. This can be provided by taking the turtle outside daily for a few minutes or by using an artificial ultraviolet light (black lights are best) on top of the aquarium during the day. These lights can be purchased from electrical supply stores and nurseries.

Food and Water

Box turtles enjoy a varied diet. Fruits and vegetables, such as spinach, kale, peaches, melons, canned or frozen mixed vegetables, and other assorted greens should be offered every other day. Worms, crickets, and grasshoppers should be given regularly. Water placed in a shallow dish should be kept clean and filled at all times.

Maintenance

I suggest keeping your turtle only for a "season;" i.e., spring to fall, or fall to spring. If he is caught in early spring and released in September, he will have time to undergo normal hibernation.

If using newspaper as a substrate, remove it and clean the aquarium thoroughly at least twice each week. If you are using gravel and rocks, remove the contents and clean thoroughly once each week. Remove all uneaten food at the end of the day. Box turtles are prone to dehydration; to prevent this, he should be sprayed with a mister or given a bath daily.

Release/Disposal

Ideally, the turtle should be released at or near where he was caught. Be sure to find a place with plenty of vegetation and as far from roads as possible. If your turtle was purchased at a pet shop, be sure it is a local variety before you release it. Some pet shops import similar-looking turtles from other countries and, therefore, they cannot be released locally. If you have one of these, consult your nearest zoo or nature center for advice.

Notes and Afterthoughts

Don't let the dog play with your turtle as he considers it just a neat new chew bone.

Musk Turtles

This could be any number of species of commonly named mud and musk turtles and also called stinkpot turtles. They rarely exceed five inches in length and are usually dark-colored, brown, black, green, or tan. They are fresh water animals which are primarily carnivorous. These turtles have scent glands at the back of their tails and may give off a strong odor when handled.

Acquisition and Handling

These turtles may be literally picked up in almost any slow moving shallow body of water where they forage for food during the daylight hours. They will attempt to bite when first caught but will calm down and become more and more docile as time passes. They may also be easily caught by using an old crawfishing method which consists of a cane pole, a fishing line, and a piece of raw meat tied at the end of the string. These turtles aren't the brightest in the world and will grab the meat and refuse to let go even when hauled up onto the pier. Dangle the meat two or three inches beneath the surface of the water. Then wait!

Cage and Habitat Materials

Unless you have a real propensity for natural surroundings, all the musk turtle requires is water! This can be supplied by simply filling a 10-gallon aquarium or plastic sweater box to a depth that will just come over the top of the turtle's shell. A flat rock will supply a place to haul out! Look at the setup in Fig. 22.

Temperature/Light/Humidity

Being reptiles, cold water makes turtles sluggish and may give them the urge to hibernate. They will refuse to eat because they cannot digest their food properly. The water temperature should be 70 and 78 degrees Fahrenheit. Use the water heater shown in Fig. 15. These turtles do not tend to bask except at the surface of the water, so light is not a critical factor.

Food and Water

To avoid fouling the water, you need to find out how much and exactly what your turtle prefers to eat. You should try a variety of foods, and here is a partial list: worms, crickets, moths, small pieces of raw meat (no hamburger!), chopped greens, aquarium plants such as Anachris, snails, small slugs, cricket frogs, and bits of liver.

You may use tap water for habitat. The chlorine will not hurt the turtle and will help control bacterial buildup.

Maintenance

The water will need to be changed every three or four days or more often if you accidentally overfeed. Wash and rinse the habitat using a mild detergent.

Release and Disposal

You should try to release the turtle at or near the place you found it. Do not release the turtle in cold weather spells or in a place where he is not used to, i.e., don't release a southern specimen in a northern region.

Notes and Afterthoughts

Do not put different-sized turtles together as they will fight and nip off appendages! A good rule to follow is one turtle per two gallons of water.

Painted Turtles

The painted turtles get their name from their beautiful and interesting patterns of red, yellow, black, and olive. They live chiefly in shallow water and grow to a length of five to seven inches. They have a unique camouflage situation in that long streams of algae grow from their shells making them hard to see. The adult males have very long nails on the front feet; the females' nails are somewhat smaller in size. Painted turtles range from coast to coast, through the northern states and southern Canada. They are the only basking turtles in the northern United States.

Acquisition and Handling

Painted turtles may simply be picked up in shallow water at a lake's edge and are sometimes available through the pet trade. They are usually not biters, but to be on the safe side, always pick them up in a way to avoid the nipping end (the mouth)! Their necks are not long enough to reach back more than an inch from the edge of the front of the shell. Avoid capturing newborn (under one inch) because they do not do well in captivity, even for a short period of time.

Cage and Habitat Materials

The standard 10-gallon aquarium or plastic sweater box makes an excellent habitat. You should also supply a flat rock to allow these turtles to haul out occasionally. See the illustration in Fig. 22.

Temperature/Light/Humidity

Room temperature, between 70 and 78 degrees Fahrenheit, will suffice. Painted turtles are basking turtles and require periods of direct sunlight to ensure proper vitamin utilization and absorption. You can place the entire habitat in indirect light outdoors for one or two hours a day. Artificial lighting may be supplied with a fluorescent black-light tube. This should be on a timer approximately twelve hours on and twelve hours off. A heat light, shown in Fig. 8, should be directed toward the basking surface, and the surface temperature should be between 88 and 92 degrees Fahrenheit.

Food and Water

The painted turtle is an aquatic turtle that moves from being an insectivore as a baby to a vegetarian as an adult. Offer a variety of foods such as insects, worms, minnows, guppies, bits of green leafy vegetables (no lettuce), and aquarium plants such as Elodea. You can also feed them semi-moist cat food in pellet form. You should feed the turtle small amounts at least every other day. Fill the habitat to a depth of about one-half inch over the turtle's back. You can use tap water.

Maintenance

It is important to keep the water clean; it should be changed at least twice a week or as needed. This is another turtle that prefers to eat underwater.

Release and Disposal

These are definitely hibernating turtles. Assuming this is a temporary captive, you do not want to keep him over a winter. Release him near the area where he was found in the very early autumn.

Notes and Afterthoughts

Supervise little people very closely when they are handling these turtles as they can bite real hard.

Pond Sliders (Red-eared)

Pond sliders are almost totally aquatic and are the most common turtle in the southern half of the United States. They get their name from a red flag-shaped mark on either side of their heads just behind their eyes. The rest of their presence can best be described as green. Beginning some- where in middle age, these turtles start to turn black. The older they get, the harder they are to identify. The red- eared pond sliders prefer quiet water with a muddy bottom and a profusion of vegetation. They bask on logs or other projections above the water or in masses of floating plants. They seldom haul out on banks unless it is time to lay eggs. These turtles have long been popular in the pet trade, although it is illegal to sell a turtle with a shell length under four inches in length.

Acquisition and Handling

Wherever there are students, there are red-eared pond slid- ers. They are usually apprehended while being questioned about why they are crossing the road after a rain. Or they can be simply picked up in shallow water along ponds and streams. They are nippy but you can avoid being bitten by simply staying away from the front end of the turtle. Their necks are not long enough to reach past the front edge of their shell. Avoid capturing babies because they do not do well in captivity even for a short time.

Cage and Habitat Materials

The standard 10-gallon aquarium arranged as you see in Fig. 2 will do for one turtle. The water should be changed every third day or so. You may use tap water.

Temperature/Lighting/Humidity

They do well at room temperature. Lighting may be a prob- lem. Sliders are basking turtles and require periods of direct sunlight to remain healthy. This can be accomplished by placing the entire habitat outside in a position that allows sunlight to cover perhaps half of the aquarium floor. Glass filters out the needed ultraviolet rays.

Food and Water

These turtles progress from being insectivores as babies to vegetarians as adults. The key to proper nutrition is to offer a variety of foods. Here is a partial list: insects, worms, goldfish, minnows, bits of green leafy vegetables, and aquarium plants such as Elodea which may be purchased in pet shops. You can also feed them semi-moist cat food in pellet form, not from cans or dry mixes.

Maintenance

It is important to keep the water clean. Remove all uneaten food after an hour or so. You may find that your turtle prefers to eat on the dry land while others may want to eat underwater. Change the water when it becomes cloudy.

Release and Disposal

It is especially important that these turtles be allowed to hibernate. I would suggest capture in early spring and release in late summer. Preventing them from hibernating might cause various health problems.

Notes and Afterthoughts

They can bite pretty hard so keep an eye on small fingers. Supervise closely all handling.

Snapping Turtles (Common)

The common snappers are large freshwater turtles with a short temper and a long tail. They are often confused with the alligator snapping turtle. The main difference being that common snapping turtles measure from eight to ten inches long, and the alligator snapping turtles measure up to three feet and may weigh up to 250 pounds. It is difficult to tell the difference when they are very young. The adult common snappers may weigh from ten to thirty-five pounds, although a captive fat one can get up to eighty pounds. They are ugly in both appearance and disposition and are easy to recognize by the large head, small breast plate (plastron), and long tail which is sawtoothed along the upper edge much like a dinosaur.

Acquisition and Handling

Any permanent body of fresh water, large or small, is a potential home for the snappers. They rarely bask as most turtles do, and underwater they are usually inoffensive. They pull in their heads when stepped on. They often dig

themselves into the mud with only the head and eyes showing. On land they may strike repeatedly. Small and
medium-sized specimens may be carried by their tails. Keep
the belly side toward your leg. Small turtles may be handled gently and carefully and are usually not prone to
biting. Fear not, for they do not hold on until it thunders!

Cage and Habitat Materials

Snapping turtles should be short-term captives and all that
is necessary is a container with water. This can be supplied
simply by filling a 10-gallon aquarium or plastic sweater
box to a depth that will just come over the top of the turtle's shell. A flat rock should be supplied, as these turtles
like to rest their front quarters on the edge of a rock out of
the water. If you fill the habitat with sand or mud so they
can burrow, you may never see them because they will
never come out of the mud. It will be messy to keep clean
and will become stagnant after a short period of time.

Temperature/Light/Humidity

The water temperature will regulate the activities of these
turtles; therefore, it is best to try to keep the temperature
around 75 degrees Fahrenheit. These are not basking turtles
except at the surface of the water. Light is not a critical factor. Heat may be supplied by either an overhead spotlight
as seen in Fig. 8 or by the portable lamp at one end of the
habitat as shown in Fig. 11.

Food and Water

The common snapping turtles are omnivorous and food
includes various small aquatic animals such as fish, frogs,
crayfish, carrion, and surprisingly, a large amount of vegetation. The vegetation may be supplied by purchasing
common water plants at the pet shops, for example,
Camomba and Anachris. These plants will remain alive for
a period of time. Food may be offered every other day and
removed at the end of the day so as not to foul the water.

The carrion I mentioned could be in the form of small pieces of lean red meat. Offer these with a pair of forceps and be careful as the snap is sometimes misguided and may get a finger!

Tap water may be used for these animals as the chlorine will keep algae growth and bacteria to a minimum.

Maintenance

The water will need to be changed every three to four days. No more than a week should pass between cleanings. Uneaten food must be removed immediately. The entire habitat should be dismantled and cleaned thoroughly at least once each week. Do not use soap in cleaning the aquarium as these chemicals may cause harm to your turtle.

Release and Disposal

You should try to release these turtles into their natural habitat at or near the place you found them. Do not release these turtles in cold weather or in a place that they are not used to.

Notes and Afterthoughts

It is a good idea to keep these animals by themselves simply because they are prone to snap at other turtles and may remove a foot or a tail. They are quite aggressive.

Soft-shelled Turtles

These animated pancakes are among the fastest moving of all the turtles. They are powerful swimmers and can run on land with startling speed. The shell is soft and leathery and no scales are evident. All the species are aquatic. They bask on shore but only a short distance from the water where they will slide or dash into the water in a second. They like to lie buried in the mud or sand in shallow water with only their eyes and snout exposed. They range in size from seven to twenty inches.

Acquisition and Handling

Soft-shelled turtles can be picked up in almost any slow moving tributary. They should be approached with caution and grabbed from the rear of the shell simply because they are very good at biting. Their extremely long necks can sometimes reach as much as three-fourths of the shell length to the back. You must also be aware of the long claws that will immediately begin to rake at your fingertips. Hold firmly because they are quite active when first picked up.

Cage and Habitat Materials

Assuming these will be temporary captives, the simplest aquarium setup will suffice. A 10-gallon aquarium or plastic sweater box can be filled up to a depth of one inch with aquarium gravel that can be obtained at the pet shop. You may then fill the container to a depth of about twice the height of the turtles' backs which allows them to breathe simply by sticking their heads above the water surface. You should also include a flat stone that is at least as large or larger than the turtles themselves. This allows them to get out of the water to bask or sun themselves when required. A 10-gallon aquarium will house nicely two small turtles or one that is over four inches. Anything larger than that will require a bigger container, and you probably don't want to keep it as a permanent pet anyway.

Temperature/Light/Humidity

A word about "cold-bloodedness" here will be of use. Turtles are pretty well regulated in their behavior, feeding, and so forth by their surrounding temperature. At 65 degrees Fahrenheit and below they become lethargic and won't eat and will not move very much. The optimum temperature would be between 75 degrees and 80 degrees Fahrenheit. This optimum may be accomplished by placing the entire aquarium setup in direct sunlight for at least two hours a day. If this is impractical, the aquarium heat light in Fig. 8 should be arranged so that the basking rock is in part directly under the bulb. The rock should be large enough so that the turtle can select that part of it just the right distance from the bulb to suit itself. Water from the tap at about the same temperature that it is replacing is good to use. Turtles do not need aged water as do other tropical animals and fish. Chlorinated water helps to prevent bacterial and fungal infection.

Food and Water

Their food should be primarily meat. This may be such things as lean, raw table meats, fish, shrimp, earthworms and small aquarium snails. In addition, you can feed them small kibbled dog food or commercial turtle food in the

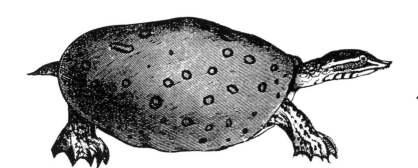

form of pellets, *not* ant eggs or dried insects, which are use-less. Most aquatic turtles will eat some plant material as well. Plant food is most easily provided in the plants sold for aquarium fish. Cabomba and Anachris are the least expensive and they'll stay alive until eaten. They like craw-fish, and your students shouldn't have a hard time finding some. They should be fed every other day.

Maintenance

Uneaten food should be removed at the end of the day so as to not cloud the water. If you do not choose to set up an elaborate filtration system, the water will need changing at least twice a week. The entire system should be dismantled and thoroughly cleaned every two weeks. Do not use soap when cleaning. Warm water and a plastic scrubber will suffice.

Release and Disposal

Release them in the same area where you got them. If this is not possible, try to release them in an area where the environmental conditions are about the same. Do not release them in fall or winter, as they might not survive the sudden changes in temperature.

Notes and Afterthoughts

You'll know when you have had these turtles for too long; their hip bones will begin to show through the shell.

Tortoises

Tortoises make fascinating and interesting pets and may live 50+ years and become quite adorable. Care must be taken in obtaining an animal because most tortoises in the United States are endangered species and therefore illegal to own. Pet shop varieties are usually the Greek tortoises or the South American red-foot tortoises and they make wonderful pets.

Acquisition and Handling

Most tortoises can be found for sale in various places such as pet shops, classified ads, or some veterinarian bulletin boards with a supply of information. Tortoises should always be handled with care, picked up from both sides, and held parallel to the ground. Don't ever turn them over on their backs or hold them upside down, as this action may cause some internal injuries.

232 • Chapter 10

Cage and Habitat Materials

Tortoises require and do best in as much space as they can
be given. A fenced-off area in a backyard or even in a large
room will suffice, and as I said, the bigger the better. They
enjoy roaming and grazing and hiding, and your habitat
should provide areas for all of these activities. Substrate for
indoors should be multi-layers of newspapers that have
aged for a period of time. Beware of sawdust, wood chips or
shavings as these may be eaten along with the food items
and can cause health problems.

Temperature/Light/Humidity

As reptiles, the temperature is very important in the health
of these animals. They prefer as much warmth as they can
get. Set up a hot spot as well as a cool area and offer the tortoise an opportunity to move to their desired place. Light is
also a critical factor in that they require unfiltered ultraviolet rays to properly utilize vitamins. Therefore, in an
outdoor habitat, there should be sunny spots as well as
shady spots throughout the day. They should be brought in
during cool evenings and, of course, during the winter
months. If they are kept indoors, two types of lights should
be provided. First, an infrared or a heat lamp, forming a hot
spot in one area of the habitat. The temperature should be
somewhere between 85 and 90 degrees Fahrenheit. Second,
ultraviolet light may be provided by use of a fluorescent
black light. This black light should be on a timer or turned
on and off, no more than twelve hours on and twelve off.
Although tortoises are desert-dwelling creatures, they do
require and enjoy some moisture. It is a good idea to bathe
your tortoise in tepid water once or twice a week. A large
shallow walk-in water dish will provide a bathing area and
your tortoises will use it frequently.

Food and Water

Tortoises are primarily vegetarians and a healthy salad
should be provided at least every other day. I will give you a
short list of some of the ingredients you may use. Spinach,

carrot tops, kale, grapes, peaches, plums, soft pear, semi-moist dog or cat food, fruit cocktail, and mushrooms are good. They also enjoy earthworms, crickets, and June beetles. The fruits and vegetables should be diced, chopped, and offered in a flat plate or bowl. Water should be supplied in a low-edged dish large enough that the tortoise can climb in and be surrounded completely. Avoid using too deep a bowl as they might slip in, be unable to get out, and drown!

Maintenance

Change substrate at least three times a week. In the outdoor habitat, dried fecal material and uneaten food should be removed daily. The water dish should be drained and cleaned and refilled on a daily basis.

Release and Disposal

You cannot release your tortoise, especially if it is an exotic breed, in the wild. Start calling and begin with your local zoo; they might have a list of people or herpetological organizations that might be willing to give your tortoise a home. Check also with local nature centers and last but not least, a high school science teacher.

Notes and Afterthoughts

Be careful with tortoises and dogs. The dogs seem to consider tortoises and turtles as chew bones and they can cause serious damage.

Chapter 11
WORMS AND MOLLUSC

Worms: Various invertebrates, as those of the phyla Annelida, Nematoda, or Platyhelminthes, having a long, flexible rounded or flattened body, often without obvious appendages.

Mollusc or Mollusk: Members of the phylum Mollusca; largely marine invertebrates.

Earthworms

Earthworms are not only useful as food items for other pets, but are a good species for classroom study activities concerning behaviors such as reaction to light, heat, temperature, and other phenomenon.

Acquisition/Handling

Worms can be purchased at any bait shop. Handling should be kept to a minimum as this interrupts their slime covering and makes them susceptible to infection and dehydration. During the warm months, you can dig them up in most damp areas, especially under garden stones and pieces of lumber that have been left out for a long period of time.

Cage and Habitat Materials

The 10-gallon aquarium is the most practical container for your worm farm. For a substrate, mix equal amounts of humus and sphagnum moss. Fill the aquarium to a depth of eight to ten inches. Cover the surface soil with damp paper towels, sphagnum, or even leaves.

Temperature/Light/Humidity

The ideal temperature is between 65 and 75 degrees. If your earthworms will be a short-term project, they may be kept in the refrigerator and will stay alive for several weeks. Check occasionally to see that there is sufficient moisture in the container. Too much moisture is fatal to earthworms, so you don't want mud.

Food and Water

You must of course maintain the moisture at all times. Your earthworms will eat a variety of food substances. A partial list of these will do: cereals, bread crumbs, tea and coffee grounds, pulverized dry dog and cat foods. These materials should be thinly sprinkled over the top of the soil under the paper towels about once each week.

Maintenance

As your paper towel covering disintegrates, just remove and add a fresh layer. Check moisture daily and avoid build-up of foodstuffs. If it forms a crust, you are feeding too much.

Notes and Afterthoughts

Turn the soil occasionally to prevent stagnation.

Land Snails

Land snails are mollusks, members of a large ancient group of soft-bodied invertebrates. They are close relatives of the clams, mussels, squids, and the octopus. They are slow moving marvels with determination and liquid beauty. They are also fun to watch.

Acquisition and Handling

Snails of various kinds can be purchased at the pet shop. They can also be collected from almost all moist soil areas. At night they may be found crawling about. During the day they hide beneath rotting logs and large flat stones in various kinds of debris. Handling snails can be tricky because they adhere very tightly to smooth, flat surfaces. You may need to slide them to an edge of the surface to remove them.

Cage and Habitat Materials

Any habitat containing snails must be covered to prevent their escape. I have found a wide-mouth gallon jar, either glass or plastic, makes an excellent home for land snails. Soil, to a depth of an inch, should be provided and kept moist to allow burrowing and perhaps laying eggs. You can provide branches, small rocks and other decorations that the snails would enjoy climbing on.

Temperature/Light/Humidity

Land snails can be maintained adequately at room temperature and with available light. Moisture is very important; if
it becomes too dry the snails will become too dry and will
attach themselves to the sides of the container and become
dormant. The soil should be kept moist but not wet.

Food and Water

Land snails will eat a variety of foods, but a diet of lettuce,
shredded carrots, and thin slices of apples or celery will
keep them healthy. These snails can go for several days without eating if they have adequate moisture. They require no
special attention over weekends and holidays. The soil substrate may be sprayed lightly with water several times a
week to maintain proper humidity.

Maintenance

It is necessary to remove uneaten food to prevent it from
rotting and fouling the container. Try to avoid a build-up of
fungus and clean the container as needed.

Release and Disposal

Those snails collected locally are no problem. Simply put
them back where you found them. The pet shop variety
should not be released into the wild unless you know something of their original habitat. You might call the pet shop
and ask if they would like them back, or contact a local
museum or nature center. Call a school teacher and ask if
they would like to maintain your colony.

Notes and Afterthoughts

Give your snails some crawling room. One snail in four
square inches of space will do nicely.

Mussels, Fresh Water Clams

The clam is the animal observers' dream. To watch them use their foot to pull themselves along through the gravel and see the water being sucked in one end and blown out the other is remarkable to behold. Although they are short-term captives, they will hold your attention their entire tenure.

Acquisition and Handling

It will be necessary to dig around in the mud along the shore of any large body of fresh water. Don't worry about being pinched as they close up immediately when they sense your presence. When handling, remember James Bond. It's OK stirred but not shaken!

Cage and Habitat Materials

The best setup for the clam is the fish aquarium. The instructions for this setup are in the Fish section. You should increase the depth of gravel to five inches. Decorations such as rocks and plants should be avoided simply because they will be disrupted and rearranged. The mud and water setup will do as well but will stagnate quickly.

Temperature/Light/Humidity

Water temperature should be maintained around 75 degrees Fahrenheit. Avoid direct sunlight as it will facilitate algae growth and you will lose sight of your captive.

Food and Water

That's gonna be tricky! Clams are filter-feeders and utilize microorganisms and single-cell plants in the water for food. To put it bluntly, you should add about one cup of pond scum to the water about twice a week. This will cloud the water immediately but will settle within the day. They will also eat active yeast cultures. Dissolve one half cube yeast in a cup of warm water. Allow it to sit for a half hour and then pour it in.

Maintenance

I would recommend you not keep this animal for more than a week, but if you do, it will be necessary to change out the entire habitat every week to ten days. Use pond water preferably or bottled water if necessary.

Release and Disposal

Put him back where you found him during the warm months.

Notes and Afterthoughts

Be careful not to overcrowd. Two to four clams per 10-gallon habitat is enough.

Slugs

On a cool fall morning I opened the back door. I held open the screen with my foot and propped both doors open with my backside since my hands were filled with three different cat foods for my finicky cat. As I bent over to position the dish to pour the food, I felt something unbelievably slimy and wet touching my fingers. I slowly moved the dish, and there it was. The slug is a mollusk and has close relatives such as the clam, oyster, and octopus. There are many different varieties of slugs in the world. Our back porch variety is the spotted golden slug. They venture out only at night because the sunlight might dry out their mucus-covered skin. These animals should probably not be kept longer than 24 hours, and any container you put them will become slimed almost immediately.

If you feed your cat on the back porch and leave the food overnight, the next morning you will see silvery trails across the porch. You have witnessed slug slime. Slugs look like large snails without a shell. The mucus enables them to slide easily and also aids in absorbing oxygen.

Acquisition and Handling
Once you've touched a slug, handling will be out of the question. Just flip them into a container with a small twig. You will find them hiding under garden stones and other material near the outside water faucet. At night they will be sliming across the wet leaves searching for food.

Cage and Habitat Materials
You will only want to keep these for a day or two in a plastic shoe box or gallon jar as illustrated in Fig. 5 and Fig. 6. The problem is that the mucous streak they leave will soon coat the entire container making it impossible to see them. Add to the container moistened leaves over a thin layer of soil. The habitat should remain moist at all times.

Temperature/Lighting/Humidity

Room temperature and indirect sunlight is sufficient.

Food and Water

Slugs eat decaying plant matter. They also will thrive on moist dog or cat food placed in a shallow dish. Mist the habitat once each day to maintain humidity.

Maintenance

If kept longer than a couple of days, remove all uneaten food and change the leaf litter to avoid the formation of mold.

Release and Disposal

Simply return them to the flower bed.

Notes and Afterthoughts

They love to eat pansies so you might reconsider where you release them.

Chapter 12
SICK CALL

BIRDS

Problem	Symptom	Treatment
Chills	General shakiness & trembling	Remove from any draft; warm up to 90 degrees F. Call your vet.
Enteritis	Greenish droppings, rapid weight loss, dejected appearance, stops eating.	Warm up to 100 degrees F. Start antibiotics from vet.
Feather-plucking	Bird pulls its own feathers from chest and wings.	Move cage to different scenery. Buy new toys; mist daily to ease irritation.
Moulting	Losing feathers; looks terrible.	Put cage in even temperature; mist bird daily; leave him alone—this is a natural occurrence.
Stroke or fits	Erratic jerking and trembling; holding wings spread.	None—leave alone.
Diarrhea	Thin, waterery stools.	Remove greens from diet.

REPTILES

SNAKES

The most common concern I hear from teachers and parents is that they can't get their snake to eat. I will address the most common reasons for this:

New to Habitat Allow a month or two for familiarization with a new habitat before you really expect a lot of feeding behavior from a snake.

Too Hot — Too Cold A cold snake might eat a mouse but then he will regurgitate it because the temperature is incorrect for proper digestion. If the temperature is too high, he will simply refuse to eat, and his behavior becomes extremely hyperactive.

Ecto/Endoparasites These conditions will need correcting before the animal will have an interest in food.

Shedding When the eye covers cloud, signaling onset of the shedding process, a snake usually has no interest in food. Try again when the skin has been shed.

Insecurity Some snakes require a place to hide and rest and may be too nervous in the open to accept food. Provide an enclosure which is described under "Cage and Habitat Materials" in the text.

Technique Most snakes don't really care how you dangle the mouse, but some are quite touchy and particular. If a wiggle of the mouse doesn't work one way, try some other way. *Do not offer your snake live food!*

Problem	Symptoms	Treatment
Mites	Pinhead-sized insects found beneath folds of skin under the chin, and causing a raised scale condition around the eyes.	* Need more room, see following page.
Intestinal worms	Weight loss, loose skin, lethargic, blood-tinged mucus and stool.	Find the right vet!
Dry shed	Incomplete shed, flakiness, extreme dry skin.	Put snake in bag of coarse cloth; keep bag wet for 8 to 12 hours, or allow snake to remain completely immersed for 6 to 8 hours.
Burns	Exposed scale damage and exposed flesh; open wound.	Clean with hydrogen peroxide and treat topically with antibacterial wound dressing such as Panolog or Furacin ointment.
Scale blister	Fluid-filled areas of scales.	Reduce humidity; do not allow soaking, prevent by placing large rock in water bowl.
Mouth rot	Raised lip, swollen gums, cheesy material around teeth.	Use cotton swab and bathe entire mouth with hydrogen peroxide. Then apply Betadine solution; if condition persists, consult veterinarian for systemic antibiotics.

* Put a slice of no-pest strip in a jar with holes in the top. The holes should be punched from the inside out so the sharp edges will not harm the snake. Leave this jar in the aquarium for at least 22 days. This will kill all adults and future hatchlings.

No-pest strips may not be sold in your area so you might need to go to procedure two. Fill a container, such as a bucket with lid, with about two inches of tepid water. Immerse the snake for 10 to 15 minutes at least twice each day for two days. Only his nose should be sticking out of the water. Are you confused yet? Then repeat this procedure once each day for one week. Wait, you are not through yet! Wait one week and then repeat the process all over again. Do this for at least one month. This will drown all adults and their offspring.

Mites can burrow through eye tissue and cause blindness and eventual slow death. Don't give up.

LIZARDS

Most all of the ailments that occur in captive lizards can be attributed to improper husbandry. Always think clean!

Problem	Symptoms	Treatment
Dehydration	Skin dried, scaly appears loose, loses elasticity.	Large water pan for soaking; mist with atomizer frequently.
Blister disease	Fluid-filled blisters; browning of belly scales.	Lessen humidity; avoid wet substrate. If pus is present, apply antibiotic ointment such as Panolog.

Problem	Symptoms	Treatment
Starvation	Loss of muscle tone; sunken appearance in face, shriveled skin, bones become prominent.	May require tube feeding with high calorie, low-bulk formula which can be obtained from your veterinarian.

TURTLES

The key to turtle health in almost all situations is the availability of sunlight. You should go to great lengths to see that they get sunlight on a daily basis.

Problem	Symptoms	Treatment
Respiratory infections	Clear nasal discharge; loss of normal swimming equilibrium, laying with head extended & resting with head on surface.	Injections of ampicillin or chloromycetin. See your veterinarian.
Abscess	Tumorous growth, usually on the side of the head.	Abscess should be lanced, flushed with hydrogen peroxide, swabbed daily with Betadine solution. See your veterinarian.
Shell deformity	Irregular shell growth or softness of scales.	Change to more balanced diet, supply sufficient ultraviolet light.
Swollen eyes	Eyes enlarged and completely closed; a pus-like substance oozes out.	Swab with antibiotic (tetracycline) solution daily until condition clears. Put in sunlight to help speed healing.

MAMMALS

The key to healthy small mammals is a simple adherence to general good husbandry practices. The key words here are clean, dry, draft-free, nutritionally sound, and careful handling. This will be a compound of general health defects that might occur in mice, rats, gerbils, hamsters, guinea pigs, and rabbits. You should consult resource materials in any of these particular animals before you spend time and money at the veterinary clinic.

Problem	Symptoms	Treatment
Small cuts and skin damage	Bleeding from somewhere.	Usually best left alone.
Teeth	Teeth are way too long.	Clipping teeth is a veterinary function. Provide gnawing blocks to promote wearing away.
Wet tail	Hair around anal opening never dries out. Loss of appetite, ears laying down.	Isolate animal; see your veterinarian.
Diarrhea	Liquid stools.	Diet incorrect; change food items.
Baldness	Hair loss.	Try yeast tablets or diet change.
Fleas and ticks (not usual)	Scratching, biting at skin.	Sprinkle any type of flea powder around the nest area every 4 days. Change bedding between applications.

FISH

Take great care to inspect the fish before you spend the money. Most pet shops will guarantee the health of their fish if you follow accepted care procedures.

Problem	Symptom	Treatment
Checklist: Water pollution, insufficient oxygen, chlorine in water, too cold, acid level too high	Fish are listless, refuse food, are generally inactive.	Review checklist, correct problem.
Shakes	Fish's body moves from side to side with no forward progress.	Change water or raise temperature.
Ick (parasite)	Body covered with small white dots.	Raise water temperature to 85 degrees F. Add latest chemical treatment to be purchased at the pet store. Follow label directions.

Chapter 13
NOTES AND NO'S ABOUT WILD MAMMALS AND BIRDS

There will be those times when your student will bring home an animal that did not necessarily follow him. The story will go that it was absolutely imperative he "rescue" the animal from certain death. That is sometimes the case and I want to offer some suggestions about how to maintain the animal until qualified, legally permitted help can be found. It is never a good idea to keep a wild mammal or bird as a pet.

Does this animal need saving?

Guidelines

Yes, if:

- A baby animal in the path of traffic or jaws of a dog or cat
- A featherless or hairless animal
- Obviously sick or injured (caution: children are not to touch, just to report the location)

No, if:

- Up a tree during the day or trapped in a trash can or garage (just leave the exit open and go away)
- Dashing around in the bushes or trees
- Feathered bird squawking in the grass

NOTES: Injured or sick animals may have distemper or rabies, and you should notify animal control to prevent bites or further injury. Do not attempt to feed orphaned, sick, or injured babies because in their stressed condition that simple act might kill them. They can't die of starvation right away but water is important. The first question you should ask the expert is how to give it a drink.

Small mammals and birds can be placed in a shoe box with air holes punched with a pencil (before you put the animal in!!!). A rubber band (or tape) at each end will secure the top.

Call the local zoo or nature center and ask about permitted wildlife rehabilitation in the area and get the animal there as soon as possible!

There will be times when you cannot transfer the animal right away and it will be necessary to provide a little first aid. These measures are only intended to keep the animal alive until trained help is found. I hope these limited instructions don't raise more questions than they answer.

BIRDS

It will be difficult to generalize care of baby birds without first dividing them into groups. That will make it necessary for you to determine pretty nearly the kind of bird you have rescued. There are two major categories that even people who know nothing about birds can recognize:

Altricial   These birds are born naked, blind, and helpless. Some examples are blue jays, mockingbirds, sparrows, grackles, doves, pigeons, and others. These animals are nest-bound and will be for two to five weeks, depending upon the species.

Precocial   These birds come into the world furry-feathered, running, and eating. Examples of these birds include: chickens, turkeys, ducks, quail, killdeer, and others. These animals require maternal care only as far as protection goes.

Here are some general procedures that can be associated with members of both groups of birds. Keep in mind that these are first-aid measures and will only maintain the animal until experienced help can be located.

Artificial Nest: For altricial birds, a shoe box lined with soft tissue paper is good. Poke holes in the box for ventilation.

CAUTION: Do NOT save the natural nest for use because it harbors all manner of little vermin, parasites, and other creepies! For precocial birds, a cardboard box at least two by two feet lined with bath towel or floor mat carpet will do. Note: Do not use a slick surface lining because the baby cannot get his footing and this may cause his legs to spraddle.

Regulate Body Temperature: You will need one of the following materials to maintain heat required by baby birds of all types. These items include heating pad, heat lamp, or hot water bottle and also keep the hair dryer handy.

For altricial birds, place the heating pad beneath one end of the shoe box. Put the setting on low and place a thermometer in the warm end of the box. Shoot for something between 80 and 90 degrees Fahrenheit. For precocial birds, affix your light to one corner of the box in such a way that the floor beneath is maintained at somewhere between 80 and 85 degrees Fahrenheit. Use no more than a 40-watt bulb and adjust the temperature simply by moving the light closer or farther away.

NOTE: If you have more than one precocial bird in the box, take care not to focus the light on a food or water container, as these birds will gather and huddle and may trample or suffocate each other.

Feeding

Formula: For altricial birds, a high-protein canned cat or dog food or dry food that has been soaked to soften is good. For precocial birds, corn meal, crumbled crackers, whole wheat bread, wheat germ, crushed bird seed, or unsalted shelled sunflower seeds that have been mashed will do.

Method: For altricial birds, almost any motion near the box will cause the babies to gape. They will open their mouths to await food. Roll the food into a small ball and impale it on the blunt end of a broken toothpick or cotton swab. Place the food ball at the back of the bird's throat and this will stimulate him to swallow. For precocial birds, sprinkle the food in one corner of the floor of the box or put it in a flat container such as jar lid.

Frequency: Altricial birds should be fed every thirty minutes to an hour during daylight hours. Precocial birds should have food available at all times.

NOTE: Doves and pigeons require a little different procedure. They are known as crop feeders and actually remove partially digested foods from their mother's crop by inserting their beak down the mother's throat. It will be necessary to blend the altricial bird diet with boiled or distilled water to make a slurry. Cut the end off a plastic eyedropper and place this food-filled dropper to the beak of the bird.

MAMMALS

Artificial Nest: Again, the shoe box is the best all-round small, dark, safe enclosure for babies. Punch multiple holes in the lid and sides for ventilation. Line the box with soft cloth or tissue.

Regulate Body Temperature: Unfurred young animals cannot regulate their body temperature and can become hypothermic (too cold) after as little as 45 minutes to an hour after being exposed to surrounding temperature. Being too cold will affect sucking reflexes and digestion. The best method of raising poor body temperature is to immerse the baby in tepid water (this is what you can feel on your wrist). Massage gently and dry immediately under a heat lamp or hair dryer. You may also use heat lamps, heating pads, or hot water bottles. Raise the surrounding temperature to between 85 and 95 degrees Fahrenheit.

Feeding: Baby mammals will die of dehydration long before they die of starvation. You must administer liquids immediately! Offer boiled, cooled water with an eyedropper. You might travel to the grocery store and get some Pedialyte and use that for rehydration. If his eyes are open, just give him water every three to four hours until you can get experienced help. If not, mix this:

- One small can of evaporated milk
- One can (same can) of boiled or bottled water
- One egg yolk
- One teaspoon of honey or Karo syrup

Blend or mix well and serve at room temperature. Refrigerate the remainder for future use.

OR:

The pet shop sells Esbilac, which is a dog milk substitute, and KMR, which is a kitten milk replacement. Just follow the directions on the can. They are both excellent substitute foods.

Method: As a rule, you should not lay the animal on his back to feed him because the liquid will go down his windpipe and he will get mechanical pneumonia. Hold the animal so his body is parallel with a surface, such as your knee or tabletop, and tilt his head back. If the liquid starts coming out of his nose, stop feeding and hold the animal upside-down while tapping him gently on the back.

Most baby mammals must be stimulated to eliminate waste. After feeding the baby, take a cotton ball or soft tissue and moisten with warm water. Tap the genital area of the animal gently for a few seconds. Do not rub, as it will irritate the skin. Mother does this with her tongue, but let's not discuss that!

Frequency: Feed rabbits only twice during daylight hours. Feed all others every three to five hours around the clock while they are in your care.

Your feeding apparatus will depend on the size of the baby. For the short time you have them, an eyedropper or baby bottle will do. You can purchase various sized pet nursers at the pet shop. For example, a fully furred raccoon can handle a regular-sized baby bottle nipple.

If you suspect the baby may be injured, i.e., fell from a tree, brought up by a dog or cat, etc., be sure to relay that information to the rehabilitation person.

Remember, if you attempt to raise the wild animal as a pet, one of you will come to grief sooner or later!

Index

261